W9-DFA-912

APR   2014

LEADING
WOMEN

Hillary Clinton

JEAN F. BLASHFIELD

Marshall Cavendish
Benchmark
New York

Blashfield, Jean F.
Hillary Clinton / by Jean F. Blashfield.
p. cm. — (Leading women)
Summary: "Presents the biography of Hillary Rodham Clinton against the
backdrop of her political, historical, and cultural environment"—Provided by publisher.
Includes bibliographical references and index.
ISBN 978-0-7614-4954-6
1. Clinton, Hillary Rodham—Juvenile literature. 2. Presidents' spouses—United States—Biography—Juvenile literature.
3. Women legislators—United States—Biography—Juvenile literature. 4. United States. Congress. Senate—
Biography—Juvenile literature. 5. Women presidential candidates—United States—Biography—Juvenile literature. 6.
Women cabinet officers—United States—Biography—Juvenile literature. I.Title.
E887.C55B53 2010
973.929092—dc22 [B]
2009030267

Editor: Deborah Grahame   Art Director: Anahid Hamparian
Publisher: Michelle Bisson   Series Designer: Nancy Sabato
Photo research by Connie Gardner

Cover © STR News Reuters/Reuters/CORBIS

The photographs in this book are used by permission and through the courtesy of: *Getty Images*: Roberto Schmidt, 1;
Evan Agostini, 4; Tim Boyle, 6; Hulton Archive, 18; Time and Life Pictures, 16, 20, 36; Popperfoto, 27; Getty Image
News, 43; Carlo Shiebeck, 44; Bob Daemmrich, 54; Joyce Naltchayana, 58; Dirk Halstead, 59; Stan Hondroo, 71;
Stephen Jaffe, 74; Robert Bukaty, 76; Scott Olson, 78; Jim Olson, 92; Alex Wong, 97; AFP, 102; *AP Photo*: 15; *Corbis*;
Corbis News, 89; Jeffrey Markowitz, 47; Mike Stewart, 31; Bettmann, 28; Sygma, 24.

CONTENTS

Hillary Rodham Clinton

Introduction

The Making of Hillary Rodham Clinton

A biography of Hillary Rodham Clinton could easily be part of a series about first ladies and their fascinating lives and accomplishments. Instead, this biography is part of a series about women leaders. Young Hillary Rodham had already become a significant person in her own right when she married future president Bill Clinton, and since then, her achievements have included much more than being President Clinton's wife. She became the first woman to have a real chance at being the president of the United States. She served as a U.S. senator for New York State. And, since January 2009, she has served as secretary of state, representing President Barack Obama and the United States around the world.

Hillary has her own personality, with great influence in the world. She is recognized everywhere she goes. Many people like and admire her—but almost as many dislike her. Probably not since her childhood have people who know her—as well as many who do not—failed to have an opinion one way or another about Hillary.

CHAPTER ONE

Young Hillary

HILLARY DIANE RODHAM'S LIFE STARTED in Chicago, Illinois, where she was born on October 26, 1947. She was the first child of Hugh Rodham, a supplier of curtains to hotels and business offices, and his wife, Dorothy Howell.

Hugh Rodham grew up in Scranton, Pennsylvania, a fact that Hillary would use many years later to draw votes in that state. Although his father expected him to work in the family lace-making factory, Hugh made his way into college by playing football, which opened up other possibilities to him. He settled in Chicago, where he put his physical education degree to use by joining the U.S. Navy and training new soldiers when World War II started.

In the long run, it was her mother who inspired in Hillary her curiosity about the world and her willingness to speak out. On the other hand, Hugh Rodham gave his daughter the self-discipline to pursue subjects deeply. These traits would become important to the future Hillary.

A SUBURBAN CHILDHOOD

Hillary was only three when her father decided that he had saved enough money to buy a house in the suburbs. He bought a brick house in Park Ridge, a growing town west of Chicago. Hillary's first brother, Hugh Jr., had already been born, but her second brother, Tony, was born in Park Ridge. Hillary became a typical suburban child, playing with the many postwar children in the

The childhood home of Hillary Rodham in Park Ridge, Illinois neighborhood and starting kindergarten at a local school. Her friends were all children who would later be called baby boomers because so many babies were born soon after World War II ended.

Dorothy was a homemaker, as most women were in the 1950s. She encouraged the children to read books and to exercise their imaginations. Even after the family got a television set, they rarely watched it. Instead, they read and played games. During the summers, Hillary often led the neighborhood children as they put on plays and earned money for charity by throwing carnivals.

The family spent every August at the rustic Rodham family cottage on Lake Winola in the Pocono Mountains of Pennsylvania, near Scranton. Hillary and her brothers were free to roam. They made friends with nature and with the mountain-living families.

BECOMING POLITICAL AND INDEPENDENT MINDED

By middle school, Hillary began to pay attention to politics, especially when John F. Kennedy was running for president against Vice President Richard Nixon. She had the self-confidence not to give up that interest when other girls, more interested in clothes and makeup, laughed at her. With Dorothy's help, Hillary was learning to ignore what "everyone" was doing and not to give in to peer pressure. It was also in middle school that she became best friends with Betsy Johnson (later Ebeling), who remains her best friend today.

Based on their parents' and grandparents' political choices, both Hillary and Betsy were avid Republicans, even though they couldn't vote. After Democrat John F. Kennedy won the presidential race in 1960, the two girls volunteered to help Republicans in Chicago check voter registration lists to be sure that the vote was legitimate. Her parents did not even know she had gone into Chicago when Hillary helped

HILLARY'S MOTHER

Dorothy Howell Rodham was born in Chicago. The older of two children, she basically had to take care of herself after her very young parents divorced. At age eight, she was put in charge of her three-year-old sister when the two were sent, unaccompanied, to California to her father's parents. Dorothy found little welcome from them. Her grandmother had no patience with children, and she decreed such stern rules that, at one time, Dorothy was grounded in her bedroom for a full year except when she was at school—all for going trick-or-treating with friends.

At fourteen, Dorothy ran out of willingness to be treated so harshly. She left her grandparents' home and took a job caring for children in another family, while also continuing to go to school. It was then that Dorothy learned what a loving family could be like, an example that served her well in raising Hillary and her brothers.

As an adult, Dorothy returned to Chicago in the hope of reconciling with her mother, but they did not get along. She met Hugh Rodham while working at a fabric company. They dated for five years before marrying because Dorothy was reluctant to tie her life to his abrasive and commanding personality. Once they were married, in 1942, they waited another five years before starting a family.

Dorothy Rodham knew that her children found their father difficult to live with, as she herself did. But, having experienced a broken home, she refused to consider divorce and always gave in to her husband. In an interview she later told author Gail Sheehy, "I was determined that no daughter of mine was going to have to go through the agony of being afraid to say what she had on her mind."

Dorothy Rodham appeared in a commercial for Hillary's presidential campaign. She also showed up on the campaign trail with Hillary occasionally, though she never spoke to the gathered crowds.

other volunteers knock on doors in the African-American South Side neighborhood to check names on the registration lists. She did find a few names of voters who were supposedly residing at addresses that did not exist, and she was proud of her accomplishment.

Hillary rarely had the opportunity to dress in constantly changing fashions like the other girls in her school. Her father would not spend money on new clothes until the old ones were worn out. Because Hugh refused to give the children an allowance, Hillary started working as a babysitter as soon as she was old enough to get jobs. She was only thirteen when she got her first summer job, taking care of a nearby park. During high school she worked in a store as a clerk.

With such a demanding father, the one thing Hillary could control was whether or not she wore the thick glasses she needed to see properly. She often chose not to wear them, and her friends would have to identify the people she said hi to as they passed. Hillary did not get her first contact lenses until she was in her thirties and becoming the first lady of Arkansas.

Hillary always did very well in school, especially when her father was painfully sarcastic about any grades that he considered inadequate. Both her parents helped tomboy Hillary to become reasonably good at most sports. She was very active in Girl Scouts and her Methodist church activities.

PULLED TWO WAYS

The two main influences on Hillary in high school were two men with opposing points of view. Her history teacher, Paul Carlson, was a staunch Republican and fervid anticommunist. He introduced his star pupil to the writings of conservative U.S. senator Barry Goldwater, who would later run for president.

Carlson's views were offset by the youth minister at Hillary's Methodist church, Don Jones, who arrived at the church in 1961. Jones broke with tradition and introduced the young people of Park Ridge to the radical ideas and poetry of the beatniks (the antisociety movement of the 1950s), as well as other ideas that were part of the cultural revolution but that had, until that time, bypassed Park Ridge.

Jones called Hillary's attention to one of the basic tenets of the Methodist Church: "Do all the good you can by all the means you can." He encouraged the young church members to live their faith by taking action in society. They held food drives and babysat for children of migrant workers who were harvesting the nearby fields. He also introduced them to life beyond suburbia by taking them to black churches in Chicago. There, the teenagers, both black and white, held discussions about their goals and their realities. Until then, Hillary did not realize that the lives of most black children were very different from those of she and her friends. She had had virtually no experience of meeting African Americans.

Jones took a few of the young people into Chicago to hear Dr. Martin Luther King Jr. speak. They even went backstage to meet the famous man. Hillary was stunned to learn about the civil rights movement that had been going on without her awareness. She began to study the problem of race in the United States and to develop ways to help set right the situation that she came to regard as America's greatest wrong.

The parents in Hillary's church began to object to Don Jones's teaching, and he was asked to leave. However, he has remained a friend and adviser of Hillary's throughout her life.

Hillary was sitting in geometry class on November 22, 1963, when she learned that President John F. Kennedy had been shot.

THE CIVIL RIGHTS MOVEMENT

Hillary was a child when the quest for equal rights in society for African Americans got its major impetus from the 1954 Supreme Court decision in *Brown v. Board of Education of Topeka, Kansas*. The ruling declared it unconstitutional to have separate schools for black students and white students. Since the Civil War, many states had maintained that they were providing "separate but equal" educational facilities. Now, the court said that wasn't enough. The segregation had to stop.

The following year, Rosa Parks, a maid in Montgomery, Alabama, tired at the end of a day, sat down in one of the first seats she came to on a city bus. She refused to move to the back of the bus, as a city law required. Although several black women had been arrested for the same "offense," this time black residents of the city boycotted the bus system. Coming to national notice during this months-long boycott was a local black minister, Reverend Martin Luther King Jr.

The dam had burst on laws and traditions that made black people second-class citizens in many states. But it didn't all happen quickly. Some of the changes did not occur until the 1960s, after some blacks and whites were killed in riots, though Reverend King himself always advocated that change should be brought about only by peaceful means.

When she got home, she found her mother absorbed in the television coverage. Dorothy Rodham confessed to Hillary that she was actually a Democrat and had voted for Kennedy without letting her husband know.

Hillary's direct experience of racial diversity expanded again when, after three years of high school at Maine East—a huge, all-white school—her class was transferred to Maine South. It was there that she encountered black students for the first time.

In 1964, when Hillary was sixteen, Republican Barry Goldwater of Arizona ran for president. He was famous for his book *The Conscience of a Conservative*, the topic of one of Hillary's freshman-year papers. Excited to see him running for president, Hillary became a Goldwater Girl, one of a large group of young women who couldn't vote but who helped campaign for him and often wore cowboy hats. She also arranged for her high school to hold a mock political convention. To Hillary's surprise, the teacher in charge insisted that

Hillary was not old enough to vote when she was a "Goldwater Girl" in support of Republican presidential candidate Barry Goldwater.

POLITICAL PARTIES

Because Hillary Clinton would play a role in political parties throughout her life, it is important to understand the primary differences between the two main political parties in the United States.

People who opposed slavery started the Republican Party, called the GOP (for Grand Old Party), before the American Civil War. The party gradually came to stand for conservatism, both in economics and in society. Republicans generally believe in limiting the size of the federal government, allowing businesses to control themselves, and keeping taxes low. The government may play a role in people's social lives but not their economic activities. Recently, the party also has come to support a strong military. Sometimes Republicans are referred to as conservatives, or as the right wing of politics and government. (The term *right wing* originated in France, where the legislators who supported the king sat on the right side of the assembly chamber.)

Thomas Jefferson founded the Democratic Party in 1792. Today it is regarded as the party of liberals or progressives. In general, that means Democrats believe government should play a role in people's economic lives, particularly by helping the poor, even if that requires taxes. Democrats also believe that the government should regulate businesses in order to protect individuals, the environment, and the economy. Democrats are usually referred to as the left wing of politics and government.

In reality, most Americans are neither left wing nor right wing. Instead, their beliefs fall somewhere in the middle—they are moderates.

Republican-leaning Hillary take the part of the Democratic incumbent, President Lyndon Johnson, instead of Goldwater. She had to learn to think about civil rights, poverty, and international affairs like a Democrat.

Although Hillary had been junior class president at Maine East, she lost the race for student government president at Maine South when she ran against several boys. They laughed at her for thinking a girl could be president. However, she was voted Most Likely to Succeed in her graduating class.

Hillary Diane Rodham in her senior class picture

Hillary's teachers encouraged her to go East to college. When she realized that she could escape her father's domination at an eastern school, she chose Wellesley, an all-women's college outside Boston, Massachusetts. The brochure pictures of the beautiful campus reminded her of her beloved lakes and forests of Pennsylvania.

Hillary was already well on her way to believing that the best thing anyone can do in life is to help people through public service. She has followed that belief her whole life, as she has moved from the local and college scene to the international stage.

CHAPTER TWO

Building a Future

H

ILLARY FOUND WELLESLEY RATHER terrifying at first. The other students there seemed very different—more polished, more traveled, perhaps even smarter. But finding her niche in politics, she joined the Young Republicans and decided to major in political science.

The Wellesley girls dated guys from Harvard University, and Hillary dated men who were as engaged in current affairs as she was. The big issue of the day was U.S. involvement in Vietnam.

DISCOVERING FEMINISM

Going to an all-women's college gave Hillary a chance to try things that she might not have had an opportunity to experience at a coed college. She remembered when her classmates had laughed at her for aspiring to be president of her high school student body because a boy had always held the position. But at Wellesley, there was no one to laugh. Any woman there could be anything she wanted to be.

In 1963 Betty Friedan published a book called *The Feminine Mystique*. Friedan argued that many women were dissatisfied with their lives because their identities depended on their husbands and children. They seemed to have no identity of their own beyond that of housewife. American women's reaction to the book ignited a new feminist women's movement. The first women's movement had secured American women's right to

Life magazine printed this picture of Hillary, as a future leader, when she graduated from Wellesley College in 1969.

vote in 1920. This one, starting in the 1960s and continuing today, is slowly leading to gender equality in business, government, and other areas of society.

Feminist ideas were new to Hillary and her friends, but they quickly absorbed them and ran with them. Hillary thought she might have a future in politics. She had decided that politics "was the only route in a democracy for peaceful and lasting change." She was elected president of Wellesley's Young Republican Club. This was at a time when Hillary and students like her still could not vote. The voting age was not changed from twenty-one to eighteen until 1971, after the Twenty-sixth Amendment to the Constitution was ratified.

SWITCHING PARTIES

Thousands of young men were dying in the Vietnam War. Supposedly they were protecting democratic South Vietnam from communist North Vietnam. As the death toll increased, more and more Americans—especially young people—became convinced that it was wrong for U.S. soldiers to be fighting and dying in Vietnam at all. Hillary, too, decided that U.S. involvement in the war was wrong, and she began to march in antiwar protests. Gradually, she identified with the ideas of the Democratic Party rather than her father's Republican Party, which generally supported the war.

The civil rights struggle, the Vietnam War, and the growing feminist movement—all these factors played a role in persuading Hillary that she was really a Democrat and not her father's brand of Republican. She also began to question just who she was and who she wanted to become.

Hillary's Methodist faith had shown her that social justice was an important goal. She learned that justice is part of all society and

THE EQUAL RIGHTS AMENDMENT

Since 1923, lawmakers had introduced the Equal Rights Amendment (ERA) in Congress every year. This law would add the following amendment to the U.S. Constitution: "Equality of rights under the law shall not be denied or abridged by the United States or by any state on account of sex." Only once, in 1972, has Congress approved the ERA and then sent it to the states for ratification. By 1982, three more states still had to ratify it. That has not happened.

its functions, not just in law. Poverty, racial and gender equality, and protecting the environment are aspects of social justice. She began to see that a belief in social justice was a matter of politics, not just faith, and social justice might be achieved through political action.

Hillary edged closer and closer to a political life, which she practiced by campaigning very hard to be elected president of the Wellesley College Government Association. She asked other students what changes they wanted at Wellesley and then campaigned on a platform of making those changes. It worked. To her surprise, she won. She discovered that she liked the recognition that winning elective office brought.

ADVOCATING CHANGE

Hillary turned the student government into a group advocating change on the campus. For example, the organization lobbied to admit more African-American students because there were only six in Hillary's class. When Martin Luther King Jr. was assassinated on

April 4, 1968, she organized an all-campus strike and teach-in to protest the college administration's apparent lack of recognition of the terrible event.

Hillary also began to campaign actively for Democratic presidential candidate Eugene McCarthy, who was opposed to the war in Vietnam. However, she accepted an unpaid summer internship with the Republican Party in Washington, D.C. During the summer of 1968 she became acquainted with many important people in the federal government. The job also included a trip to the Republican National Convention in Miami, Florida. Hillary worked avidly to help Nelson Rockefeller win the Republican nomination for president, but Richard M. Nixon was nominated instead.

Many students opposed sending American soldiers to Vietnam.

In the fall Hillary returned to Wellesley for her senior year. As graduation approached, the students persuaded the administration to allow a student to speak at the graduation ceremony for the first time. Hillary was chosen as the speaker.

The main speaker at the ceremony was Edward Brooke of Massachusetts, the first African American elected to the Senate since just after the Civil War. Wellesley's president, Ruth Adams, then introduced Hillary as "cheerful, good humored, good company, and a good friend to all of us." Adams said that there had been "no debate so far as I could ascertain as to who their spokesman was to be."

Hillary had spent many hours planning her off-to-the-future speech. As she listened to Brooke, however, she took note of his objections to student protests and support of President Nixon's policies in Vietnam. Hillary launched into an impromptu speech in which she chastised the United States for its involvement in the Vietnam War, as well as Brooke personally for not taking a stand against it. She thought Brooke should recognize that young people's protests were based on legitimate complaints about government and society, and they indeed had reason to be afraid for the future.

She said that the other students had encouraged her to…

Talk about trust, talk about the lack of trust both for us and the way we feel about others. Talk about the 'trust bust.' What can you say about it? What can you say about a feeling that permeates a generation and that perhaps is not even understood by those who are distrusted?

Hillary thought she was speaking just to the audience in front of her at Wellesley, but it turned out that a *Life* magazine photographer was there. Wearing thick glasses and brightly striped pants, Hillary was featured in *Life*, along with a Brown University graduate named Ira Magaziner, as prominent voices of the future. In *Living History* she writes that the reactions of other people to what she said "turned out to be a preview of things to come: I have never been as good as or as bad as my most fervid supporters and opponents claimed."

LAW SCHOOL

Hillary decided that she could best work toward social justice by entering public service or politics. The best foundation she could have for either arena was a degree in law. Hillary applied to both Harvard and Yale universities, and both schools accepted her. The programs were equally good, but a Harvard professor grumbled to Hillary that they didn't need any more women. She turned to Yale, in New Haven, Connecticut. The class she joined in the fall of 1969 had 27 women out of 235 students. When she received her law degree three years later, Hillary was one of only 7 percent of American lawyers who were women. Today, about half the nation's law students are women.

Hillary gained recognition immediately. That winter, she served as chairman of a meeting of Yale Law School students to vote on whether to join a national student strike against the expansion of the Vietnam War—"a war that should never have been waged." At a convention of the League of Women Voters, she spoke angrily after National Guardsmen killed four students at Kent State University in Ohio during a war protest on May 4, 1970. It was at that convention that Hillary met Marian Wright Edelman, who was just starting the

Children's Defense Fund, an antipoverty organization dedicated to helping children. The two women leaders would become friends and colleagues forever.

Hillary spent the next summer in Washington, D.C., where she helped Edelman investigate the lives of children of migrant workers. As she conducted her own studies and watched Senate hearings on the conditions under which migrant farmworkers lived, Hillary became persuaded to concentrate on family law.

Hillary was working in the law library back at Yale that fall when she caught a young man staring at her. Because she had noticed him staring at her before, she went up to him and said, "You know, if you're going to keep looking at me and I'm going to keep looking back, we at least ought to know each other."

The young man was Bill Clinton, a law student from Arkansas.

WHAT TO DO, WHAT TO DO

Hillary and Bill talked politics, art, ethics, and past and present and future. In the process, they fell in love. Hillary later wrote, "To this day, he can astonish me with the connections he weaves between ideas and words and how he makes it all sound like music." Bill later wrote that Hillary "was in my face from the start, and, before I knew it, in my heart."

In 1972 Hillary and Bill went to Texas to work on George McGovern's presidential campaign. They received their law degrees the following spring. The twosome celebrated by visiting the British Isles together, and it was in England's fabled Lake District that Bill asked Hillary to marry him.

She didn't say yes, but she didn't say no. She wanted time to be certain that he was the right man for her.

Hillary Rodham met Bill Clinton when they were both students at Yale Law School.

Bill and Hillary each began a new job as a full-fledged lawyer. Bill returned to Arkansas to teach at the University of Arkansas Law School and to get involved in state politics. Hillary took a job in Cambridge, Massachusetts, with the Children's Defense Fund. She loved her work. She spent her time investigating conditions under which children—particularly children with disabilities—were sometimes forced to live. She testified before Congress on what she learned and helped ensure the passage of a new law requiring public school systems to admit children with disabilities and to provide what was necessary to educate them effectively.

Hillary was fully engaged in her work, but she also missed Bill. Occasionally she visited him in Arkansas, where he was campaigning

BILL CLINTON

William Jefferson Blythe III was born in Hope, Arkansas, a year before Hillary. His father had been killed in a car accident several months before he was born. He spent his early years with his grandparents in a neighborhood that was primarily African American. It was there that he decided that segregation of the races was wrong.

When Bill was four, his mother married a Hot Springs car dealer, Roger Clinton. It wasn't until Bill was a husky teenager that he was able to confront his alcoholic stepfather and force him to stop abusing his mother. Astonishingly, he legally changed his name to Clinton soon afterward.

At sixteen, the brilliant young man was chosen to go to Washington, D.C., as part of an American Legion program called Boys Nation. He met President John F. Kennedy at the White House and decided that he, too, would go into politics. Bill graduated from Georgetown University in Washington, D.C., and won a Rhodes Scholarship to study at Oxford University in England. Upon returning to the United States, he attended Yale University Law School. It was there that he met a student from a Chicago suburb, Hillary Rodham.

to represent the state in Congress. In the meantime, Hillary took a staff position on the House Judiciary Committee inquiry into whether President Richard Nixon should be impeached, meaning charges would be brought against him that might lead to his being removed from office. The committee was investigating the president's role in a break-in at the Democratic National Headquarters and the subsequent cover-up. The offices, where Democrats were making plans that might prevent Nixon from being reelected, were located in the Watergate Apartments in the District of Columbia. The scandal became known as Watergate.

Seven days a week, for many months, Hillary joined the band of forty-four bright, young lawyers looking into every possible aspect of impeaching the president. She concentrated on studying the Constitution and what it outlined about the procedure of impeachment. The U.S. Congress had not carried out this process since President Andrew Johnson's impeachment in 1868.

Hillary hoped Nixon could be impeached for his conduct regarding the Vietnam War, not just for using his position to cover up a crime. But eventually the House Judiciary Committee approved only three articles, or specific charges, of impeachment. These articles did not include Nixon's management of the war. Within days, President Nixon resigned rather than putting the nation through the horrors of a trial. Hillary had found the work exhilarating, but she could not have known that it would mean something to her personally someday.

Hillary's job in Washington was over. With Bill still in Arkansas, she decided to accept an earlier offer to teach criminal and constitutional law at the University of Arkansas Law School in Fayetteville. It would give her a chance to get to know Arkansas better and to make a decision about whether or not to marry Bill.

THE CLINTONS TOGETHER

In Arkansas, Hillary discovered that Bill's campaign for Congress was in disarray. She immediately took charge. It was her first experience in organizing a political campaign. Despite her help, Bill lost the election that fall. He knew he would try again.

When Bill bought a house that she had seen and loved, Hillary

President Richard M. Nixon waving farewell after resigning the presidency

could no longer resist him. They were married in the living room of that home on October 11, 1975. She decided to keep her name, Hillary Rodham, instead of taking Bill's.

The next year, Hillary and Bill worked to get Jimmy Carter elected president—Bill in Arkansas and Hillary in Indiana. At the same time, Bill was elected attorney general of Arkansas. That work widened his popularity among Arkansans, and in 1978 Bill was elected governor. At thirty-two he was the youngest governor ever to serve the state. Hillary was forced to give up her job at the university because the commute from Fayetteville to the capital at Little Rock was too long. She took a job with Arkansas's prestigious firm of lawyers, the Rose Law Firm. She would remain as a partner in the law firm until 1992, when the Clintons went to the White House.

CHAPTER THREE

The Governor's Wife

H

ILLARY RODHAM AND BILL CLINTON moved into the governor's mansion in Little Rock in 1978. Hillary became the main income earner in the family since Bill earned only a relatively low state official's salary. She continued with the law firm but also worked for the Children's Defense Fund. President Jimmy Carter, recognizing Hillary's work on his presidential campaign, named her to the board of the Legal Services Corporation, a federal organization that supports free legal aid for Americans who cannot afford to hire a lawyer. The next year, when Hillary was named a full partner in the Rose Law Firm, she became the first woman to reach that level. She concentrated on intellectual property law, but she also took on, for free, legal cases involving children when there was no money to pay a lawyer.

The Clintons joyously welcomed the birth of Chelsea Victoria on February 27, 1980. Hillary loved being a mother, though none of her work on behalf of children had prepared her for the actual experience of caring for a newborn baby. She took a long leave of absence from the Rose Law Firm, and she even extended her leave, though she did some part-time work. She was unable to have more children, so she set about enjoying Chelsea and making sure not to spoil her.

Hillary and Bill became so absorbed in their new family that they left the Arkansas people out of their excitement. They did not allow the press to make an announcement of the birth for

Hillary Rodham, as first lady of Arkansas, showed American first lady Rosalynn Carter around a farmers' market.

several days. The voters didn't like that. Nor did they like the fact that Hillary still used only her maiden name.

These reactions, along with an unpopular tax, created the possibility that Bill would not win another campaign for governor. And he didn't. He lost the 1980 election to Republican Frank White.

Bill was not prepared for the loss, and he didn't quite know what to do with himself. He joined a law firm but immediately began campaigning to return to the governor's mansion. Hillary went back to work full time at her law firm.

When Bill announced that he would run for governor again in 1982 Hillary decided it might help if she legally changed her name to Clinton. As part of her image change, she began to wear contact lenses for the first time in her life. She also managed Bill's campaign in all ways.

In 1982 Bill and Hillary Clinton, with baby Chelsea, were sent back to the governor's mansion. Chelsea was raised in the mansion because Bill was reelected in 1982 and 1984. When he was reelected in 1986, it was for four years, because the Arkansas legislature had changed the governor's term from two years to four.

Hillary served as first lady of Arkansas for twelve years, as she balanced family, practicing law, campaigning, and public service. She became very involved in Bill's plan to revamp Arkansas's educational system, which was rated near the bottom in the nation. He put Hillary in charge of the state's new Educational Standards Committee. She ignored the criticism that she had gotten the job only because she was the governor's wife. Determined to learn about how education was being carried out throughout the state, Hillary visited every school district in the state and asked what they needed. She discussed education with parents, teachers, and legislators to get their ideas.

Hillary herself presented her plan for the state's schools to the

Hillary and Bill adored their daughter Chelsea, their only child.

legislature. The plan included retesting all teachers for competence and raising taxes to support better schools. Both of these ideas had their critics, but the plan became law. Within months almost 10 percent of the teachers in the state had been fired because they could not pass the competency test. In the long run, however, Hillary's plans did not lead to great improvements. Many Arkansans thought their tax money had been wasted.

Hillary's law career kept her equally busy. Sam Walton, the founder of Wal-Mart, invited her to serve on the huge corporation's board. She also was cochair of the Children's Defense Fund, which put her at the forefront of the thorny issues of laws affecting children. She compiled three editions of the *Handbook on Legal Rights for Arkansas Women*. In 1988 and 1991, the *National Law Journal* named her to its list of America's one hundred most powerful lawyers. Joshua Green, writing in *Atlantic Monthly*, described her as

 blue-chip talent through and through.

HER MARRIAGE

While Hillary was adding to her list of accomplishments, Bill was flirting with lots of women, and he had brief sexual affairs with several of them. Hillary, seeing his political future apparently in jeopardy as rumors about his behavior flew, began to wonder if she should let him go.

In the late 1980s, when it became clear that Bill was seriously in love with another woman, Hillary considered divorce. However, she kept in mind what her mother had always said about why she put up with Hillary's stiff, unsympathetic father:

 Never get a divorce—endure everything.

Dorothy Rodham had been determined to put up with anything from her husband rather than breaking up a family as her own mother had.

Bill and Hillary reached an agreement: she would stay with him and they would, together, go after the top positions available in political life. In return, he would give up extra women. Both Hillary and Bill (but especially Bill, who taught her the technique) were able to keep their difficult private lives separate from the work they had to concentrate on.

The flying rumors did not involve only Bill. As seemed to be inevitable with Hillary, some people strongly liked her, while others strongly disliked her. Some of her critics began to spread rumors about her relationship with Vince Foster, an old friend who had encouraged Hillary to join the Rose Law Firm. She had come to depend on Foster as someone to talk to when she was distressed about Bill's behavior. Those who knew both Hillary and Vince never had any doubt that the stories were lies.

TO THE NATIONAL SCENE

From his southern state base, Bill Clinton was making a name for himself in national Democratic politics. He considered running for president in 1988 but decided that the time wasn't right, especially since he would be away campaigning during Chelsea's formative years. Instead, his friend Michael Dukakis, governor of Massachusetts, asked Bill to make his nomination speech at the Democratic National Convention in 1988. Normally such speeches are quick, five-minute endorsements, but Dukakis wanted Bill to spend all the time he needed to tell the audience about him in detail.

Extraordinarily for a man who later came to be known for his great speeches, Bill was so bad that the audience chanted for him to "get off, get off," and they cheered when he said, "In closing . . ." Bill writes in his autobiography,

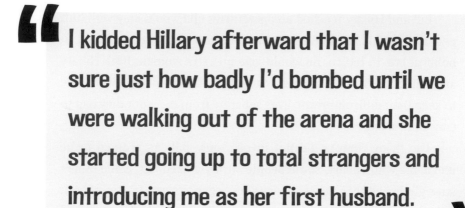

" I kidded Hillary afterward that I wasn't sure just how badly I'd bombed until we were walking out of the arena and she started going up to total strangers and introducing me as her first husband. **"**

But Bill Clinton did not run and hide. Instead, he appeared on Johnny Carson's *Tonight Show* and played the saxophone for America. Years later, Bill told a group of students,

" If you live long enough, you'll make mistakes. But if you learn from them, you'll be a better person. It's how you handle adversity, not how it affects you. **The main thing is never quit, never quit, never quit.** **"**

Bill reentered the race for governor in 1990, but his heart wasn't really in it. With Hillary's help, he managed to beat the other Democrats in the Arkansas primary. They then dove into a nasty campaign. Despite the fact that people kept bringing up Bill's sexual misconduct, he won a sixth term as governor of Arkansas.

Bill promised Arkansas voters that he would serve out his full term, but Hillary had other ideas. She had seen that President George H. W. Bush was not doing very well in the polls, but no Democrats appeared to be ready to challenge him for the 1992 presidential election. Hillary persuaded Bill that it was his time to run for president.

CHAPTER FOUR

The National
Campaign

H ILLARY WAS WITH BILL CLINTON in late 1991 when he announced that he would run for president. He said he would offer "leadership that will restore the American dream, fight for the forgotten middle class, provide more opportunity, demand more responsibility from each of us and create a stronger community in this great country of ours."

"Bill who?" asked most Americans. The press called him an obscure but colorful politician from a southern state and gave him little chance of succeeding. But he began to prove his popularity in the first state elections. Hillary helped him prepare speeches, did research, and had Bill bounce ideas off her.

Before starting the campaign, Hillary had had to resign all her positions—from her law firm as well as from her various boards and charities. That left her with little to be except Bill Clinton's wife. Once again, she had only two names, but this time they were Hillary Clinton, not Hillary Rodham. She called it "an odd experience" being without any of her old identity.

QUESTIONS ARISE AGAIN

Within a few weeks of Bill's announcement, the name Gennifer Flowers surfaced. In a tabloid newspaper, this Arkansas woman claimed that she and Bill had had a romantic relationship lasting twelve years, including all the years he was governor of

Bill Clinton announced that he would run for president in 1991, with Hillary and Chelsea on stage with him.

Arkansas. Bill told Hillary that there was no truth to the story, and she accepted his denial.

But the country didn't. Just weeks away from the first primary, Bill and Hillary appeared on the CBS television program *60 Minutes*. Bill denied having an affair with Flowers but admitted that he had caused "pain in my marriage." When the interviewer implied that Bill and Hillary were together only as a political arrangement, Hillary angrily made a comment that would stick with her:

 You know, I'm not sitting here, some little woman standing by my man like Tammy Wynette. I'm sitting here because I love him and I respect him and I honor what he's been through and what we've been through together.

Country music fans who liked Wynette's song "Stand by Your Man" were offended.

Hillary had learned long ago to think before speaking, so the Tammy Wynette comment was unusual for her. Steve Kroft, the newsman who interviewed the couple on *60 Minutes*, later said to Gail Sheehy, "She's tougher and more disciplined than he is. . . . She's got a ten-second delay. If something comes to her mind she doesn't

THE VOCABULARY OF PRESIDENTIAL ELECTIONS

Each political party holds initial elections to choose its nominee. Those initial elections are called primary elections when they are done by secret ballot. In a few states, such as Iowa, the parties hold gatherings called caucuses in every town, where residents have to announce publicly whom they support. Because the primary season is fairly short, many states hold their primaries all on one day, called Super Tuesday. Each party narrows its candidates down to one, who is officially named, or nominated, at the party's national convention. The general election campaign follows, and the national election takes place in November. The whole process generally takes most of a year.

think will play right, she cuts it off before anybody knows she's thinking it."

Americans were generally intolerant of questionable behavior in their politicians' private lives. Four years earlier, Senator Gary Hart had been forced out of the presidential race when an extramarital affair became public. But the Clintons' willingness to confront the issue and then to carry on as if there were no bad rumors kept Bill in the race. Hillary didn't totally ignore the stirring rumors. Speaking at a Democratic fund-raising event, she said she was there because Bill was accompanying Chelsea, then eleven, to a party for teens in Little Rock. Then she added, "I've heard so many rumors this week, I can't keep track of them. And I know you've heard them, too. . . . You may have even started some of them."

The Iowa caucuses were the first occasion for voters to notice Bill Clinton. Tom Harkin, the senator from Iowa, won, so Bill and Hillary, expecting that outcome, concentrated on the next occasion, the Democratic primary in New Hampshire. Bill lost to Paul Tsongas of Massachusetts, but he came in a surprisingly strong second, enough so that he could call himself "the comeback kid." Bill continued on to win most states on Super Tuesday. Although former California governor Jerry Brown made a strong showing, Bill earned the Democratic Party's nomination.

HILLARY AS TARGET

The primaries weren't easy. People continually brought up Bill's other women. It turned out that a woman was indeed part of the problem he had to overcome, but that woman was Hillary. From the beginning, the couple made it clear that the nation would get a "twofer," meaning that Hillary would play a role in policy making. Bill called their relationship "an unprecedented partnership" or, more casually, "Buy one, get one free!" Many Americans disliked that idea. And the media took Bill's casual comment out of context and blew it up for the public to laugh at.

From the day she chose to marry Bill, Hillary had to navigate the American people's various attitudes toward women. Within government circles, the presence of women was common and accepted. Politicians generally listened to and respected women. But the feminist movement had not yet caught on in all of the United States.

It was clear from the first that, if Bill were elected president, Hillary would be a different kind of first lady. The press scrutinized her more than any other would-be first lady. When people criticized her for thinking she could be co-president, she backed off and began to emphasize her feminine accomplishments. She talked about the life she was leading and said, "You know, I suppose I could have stayed home and baked cookies and had teas, but what I decided to do was fulfill my profession." Many women who liked baking cookies and holding teas felt Hillary was putting them down, so she was criticized again.

New York Times columnist Maureen Dowd described the reaction this way: "The Republicans are busy mining fears as old as Adam and Eve about the dangers of an assertive, ambitious woman speaking into the ear of her man."

Hillary also broke away from tradition by setting up her own campaign staff. Previously, the male candidate's staff had determined where and when his wife would appear in public. Hillary did not accept that. She knew that she would be almost as big an issue for the voters as Bill himself, so she would fight in her own way. She set about trying to demonstrate to the public that she, her marriage, and their campaign were not damaged goods.

Hillary and her advisers were astonished and dismayed at how some segments of the public reacted to her. She had worked for children's issues since law school, yet that didn't seem to be enough to draw traditional women to her. Apparently some of them did not realize that she had a child of her own, that she wasn't only a career-oriented woman.

Hillary returned to Wellesley College to give a speech that she hoped would help. She spoke up for an "integrated life." She praised women who found a balance among family, work, and service. She said, "When all is said and done, it is the people in your life, the friendships you form and the commitments you maintain that give shape to your life. Your friends and your neighbors, the people at work or church, all those who touch your daily lives. And if you choose, a marriage filled with love and respect."

New York Times writer Joyce Purnick perused many newspaper stories about Hillary during the campaign. In an article called "Let Hillary be Hillary," Purnick sums up the articles this way:

> **She will now favor soft pastels over crisp business suits. She doesn't bake cookies. She does bake cookies. She'll advise her husband. She won't advise her husband. She should advise her husband. She shouldn't. She's too aggressive, she loves children, she cares about family. She should, shouldn't, can, can't, won't . . .? . . . Even as the public learns to accept flawed candidates, it persists in demanding some idealized, elusive perfection from political wives.**

Purnick concludes,

> **Why can't political wives have real jobs, freely voice their own opinions, lose their tempers, wear glasses (gasp!), make mistakes, be soft or hard, stray from the straight and narrow, or generally mess up? Their husbands do.**

Hillary Clinton spoke at Wellesley College again while campaigning for her husband for president.

Ultimately, Bill Clinton was elected president. In 1992's election a third-party candidate, Ross Perot, received a larger share of the vote than a third-party candidate had received in many years. Perot, an Independent, received 18.9 percent of the vote, and George H. W. Bush, who was hoping for a second term, received 37.4 percent. William Jefferson Clinton received 43 percent of the vote. Bill and Hillary Clinton were on their way to the White House.

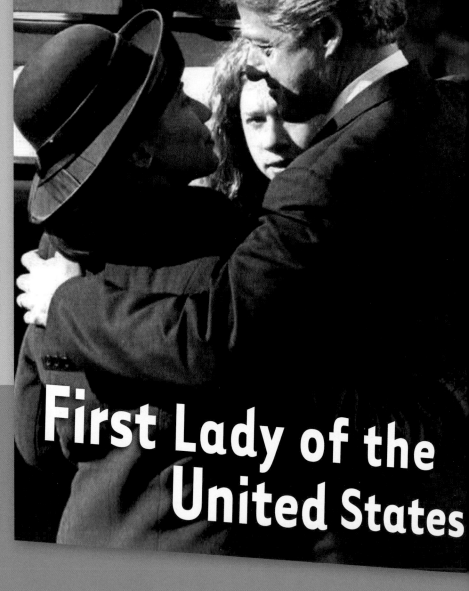

CHAPTER FIVE

First Lady of the United States

O N JANUARY 20, 1992, BILL CLINTON was sworn in as the forty-third president of the United States. At the inaugural ceremonies and balls held that evening, Hillary asked to be announced as Hillary Rodham Clinton. After years as Hillary Clinton in Arkansas, she decided to bring her maiden name back into use.

Unlike previous first ladies, Hillary Rodham Clinton established an office for herself in the West Wing of the White House instead of the more usual East Wing. The West Wing is the building where the president's Oval Office, as well as other offices of the administration, is located. Hillary's new West Wing office reflected the kind of change that both Bill and Hillary envisioned for the first lady's role.

When asked why Hillary chose a West Wing office, Dee Dee Myers, President Clinton's press secretary, replied,

Because the President wanted her to be there to work. She'll be working on a variety of domestic policy issues. She'll be there with other domestic policy advisers.

The Clinton family after Bill was sworn in as president on January 20, 1993

According to White House officials, Hillary would be in charge of creating a proposal to make health care available to all Americans.

In early 1993, when the Clintons had been in the White House only a few weeks, it became clear that Hillary's father, Hugh Rodham, was dying in Little Rock. Hillary and Chelsea went back to Arkansas to be with him in his last days.

TRYING FOR HEALTH CARE

For decades the American public has been divided on whether or not it is right for the federal government to play a role in controlling health care costs and providing health insurance. The Clintons believed that medical care is a right, not a privilege. But they knew that many corporations, medical groups, and insurance companies would fight against any plan that would guarantee health care to every American.

Bill put Hillary in charge of the task force to create a new health care program that would take care of the millions of people who could not afford health insurance. Some Washington insiders startling grumbling immediately, but Bill and his staff were delighted at their success in the election and thought they had a mandate to do anything.

Hillary worked on the President's Task Force on National Health Care Reform with colleague Ira Magaziner, the young man who, like Hillary herself, had been written up in *Life* magazine thirty years earlier. He had become a major expert in preparing strategies for corporations. Hillary and Magaziner wanted to write the legislation themselves instead of turning it over to Congress. They hoped that by keeping the workings of the task force secret, they could prevent their opponents from attacking it every step of the way before it was even unveiled.

At Bill's urging, Hillary took on the important task of reforming the American health care system.

Hillary traveled around the country, gathered information, and explored possibilities. As she had always done when approaching a new task, she studied deeply and became an expert on the subject. When testifying before Congress on health care subjects, she impressed everyone with the depth of her knowledge and the clarity of her presentations.

Some years later, Maggie Williams, her close friend and former chief of staff, said,

> **When I think of Hillary I have one enduring image... it's of her after a day of events and meetings in an elevator, her arms bursting with books and papers and briefings, all about health care, on her way to the residence. She looked extraordinarily happy.**

But too many people became involved to keep the work of the task force quiet, and the process of creating a detailed bill took too long. Dubbed Hillarycare, the bill that was finally introduced in Congress was 1,342 pages long. It was far too complicated and, by that time, too unpopular to succeed. In the meantime, another senator had introduced a different health care bill. Hillary's bill was never even brought to a vote in the Senate. Senator Robert Byrd of West Virginia disliked the way the White House tried to force it through, and he was powerful enough to stop it.

While Hillary had dug so deeply into the business of health care, she had neglected to study the politics of it. She never again failed to consider the political implications of an action.

Hillary later said that she did not take the failure of her health care plan personally, but others doubt that. She told *Atlantic Monthly*'s Joshua Green, "The fact that I was *doing* it was such a shock to the Washington system. I don't think I ever recovered from that. That was the real challenge: 'He put his *wife* in charge!'. . . I think it was very convenient to hang this all on the first lady."

After losing the battle on health care, both Clintons began to shift toward the political center. Recognizing that they could not win if they stuck to their more liberal, left-leaning ideas, they became moderates.

THE FIRST LADY ROLE

The Clintons' eight years in the White House were ones of major work on international affairs and dealing with the U.S. economy. Hillary participated in many of the decision-making processes, at least through discussions with her husband. She traveled with Bill to dozens of countries and met many heads of state.

Several years later, when Hillary was nominated Barack Obama's secretary of state, Jonathan Alter wrote,

> Hillary Clinton will be an exceptionally knowledgeable and hardworking secretary of state. She didn't just visit more than 80 countries as first lady and senator, she met all the key players and developed a complex understanding of global challenges.

Hillary and Bill were also busy raising a teenage daughter. They had chosen to enroll Chelsea in a private school called Sidwell Friends, whose staff had plenty of experience educating the children of prominent Washingtonians in a protective environment. Hillary and Bill attended all of Chelsea's school and church events, as well as her ballet recitals. A highlight was Chelsea's appearance in *The Nutcracker* with the Washington Ballet Company. In all ways, they tried to give Chelsea a normal life while protecting her from the many rumors and headlines that were making life so difficult.

SWIRLING SCANDALS

Not all the rumors and scandals had to do with Bill. Hillary experienced her share of them, in ways that would affect their entire eight-year administration.

An early scandal was called Travelgate. It started when seven longtime employees of the White House travel office were fired at one time. Upon entering the White House, the Clintons had learned that the travel office had been investigated several times for possible mismanagement, but nothing had been done. They took action. But when an Arkansas firm with links to the Clintons was given the job of arranging travel, there was a public outcry. The White House travel contract was given to another firm, and eventually, most of the seven fired employees found other jobs in the government. The former head of the office was charged in court with embezzlement, or stealing funds, but he was acquitted. It remained uncertain just what role Hillary played in the mess.

Some of the animosity toward Hillary's health care plan showed up in another scandal. These very complex issues have become known by the single name Whitewater. When working with the Rose

INDEPENDENT COUNSEL

In 1978 Congress created the position of independent counsel to investigate ethics violations in government. First called the special prosecutor, the position was an outgrowth of the Watergate scandal, which led to the resignation of President Richard M. Nixon. Many Americans thought that the person in this position had too much power—almost becoming a fourth branch of government—and the law creating the position was allowed to expire in 1999.

Law Firm in Arkansas, Hillary had met a businessman named Jim McDougal and his wife. The Clintons and the McDougals formed a partnership to invest in some undeveloped land on the White River. They called their partnership Whitewater Development. The Clintons did not know that McDougal, who ran a savings and loan bank, had become unreliable in his business dealings, and some of those deals were apparently illegal. He and his wife Susan eventually went to prison.

By the end of Bill's first year in office, enough rumors of misdeeds had floated through the capital to cause Congress to initiate an investigation. Congress appointed Kenneth Starr as an independent counsel to look into possible legal charges against the Clintons. He tried to tie together a wide range of "evidence"—Hillary's former job with the Rose Law Firm, the firing of the White House travel office employees, the conviction and imprisonment of the McDougals, a missing file of papers, and the suicide of Hillary's good friend Vince Foster, who had become a White House counselor.

In November 1994 Hillary and Bill, along with many other Democrats, were stunned at how many seats the Democrats lost in Congress in the midterm election. The Republicans gained enough seats to control both the House of Representatives and the Senate. Hillary's brother, Hugh Jr., who was running for the Senate from Florida, where he was an attorney, lost in a landslide.

Hillary knew that the attacks on the Clinton presidency would become worse. The Whitewater situation plagued her throughout her years in the White House. For months on end, seemingly new revelations questioning the first lady's ethics headlined the newspapers. Perhaps because she and Bill did not speak up publicly on the issue early on, it gradually spiraled out of control. It affected Bill's presidency and Hillary's attempt to get health care for millions of Americans. Eventually, on January 26, 1996, Hillary became the first first lady to be required to testify before a grand jury.

Hillary wrote in her autobiography that she and Bill handled the painful situation very differently:

> **We were both in the eye of the storm, but I seemed to be buffeted by every gust of wind, while Bill just sailed along. The idea of hardcore Republican partisans rummaging through our lives, looking at every check we had written in twenty years, and harassing our friends on the flimsiest of excuses infuriated me.**

At the same time that she was distracted by these difficult events, Hillary did considerable good work that didn't get much attention. In 1994 Mother Teresa, the saintly nun and Nobel Peace Prize winner from India, traveled to Washington to speak at the National Prayer Breakfast. In her speech, she looked straight at Hillary and Bill and stated that abortion is "the greatest destroyer of love and peace." Both Clintons are pro-choice, meaning that they agree with the Supreme Court decision allowing women to choose whether or not to have an abortion. Hillary, however, has always held that the government must do whatever it can to make abortions unnecessary, by, for example, supporting adoption programs. Because Mother Teresa also believed that any unwanted baby should be put up for adoption, Hillary knew that the two of them could reach common ground. And they did. Together, they created the Mother Teresa Home for Infant Children in nearby Maryland, where new mothers could take care of their newborn infants while arranging for them to be adopted. When Mother Teresa died in 1997, Hillary attended her funeral in Calcutta, India.

Hillary found joy in doing such work, but the ongoing scandals took an emotional and physical toll on her. One was the affair of Paula Jones. Jones had been a state clerk in Arkansas. In 1994 she publicly stated that when Bill Clinton was governor he had made sexual advances toward her and failed to stop when she objected. She charged Bill with sexual harassment. The Paula Jones lawsuit dragged on throughout most of the Clinton presidency. It was eventually thrown out of court because Jones could not demonstrate that she had been damaged in any way. But it was that case that eventually led to the impeachment of President Clinton.

Bill was unable to spend much time worrying about the scandals. He had to deal with both international and domestic terrorism

Hillary and Bill led a day of mourning after the destruction of the Murrah Federal Building in Oklahoma City.

during his first term in office. The World Trade Center was bombed and partially destroyed in 1993. Then, in 1995, extremist Americans bombed the Murrah Federal Building in Oklahoma City. The explosion killed 168 people, including 19 children of federal employees.

Years later, some writers looking back at the first years of the Clinton administration suggested that Republicans exaggerated into major scandals what they could have viewed as minor missteps.

SPEAKING IN BEIJING

In 1996 the United Nations held an international conference on women in Beijing, China. Almost 5,000 people representing 189 nations were there. Hillary, who had always taken women's issues to heart, attended as a representative from the United States. Some of the men in her husband's administration did not want her to speak at the conference because the United States and China were not on very good terms, but she went ahead with what she had to say.

In her speech, she said what she had always believed: "Human rights are women's rights, and women's right are human rights for one and for all. Let us not forget that among those rights are the right to speak freely—and the right to be heard. Women must enjoy the rights to participate fully in the social and political lives of their countries if we want freedom and democracy to thrive and endure."

Hillary's speech was regarded as quite controversial at the time because she took on China itself, where human rights were usually disregarded and female babies were often discarded. Hillary did what she has long done in her public speeches: she exposed to light the problems faced by the invisible and underprivileged.

A SECOND TERM

With the economy of the country doing well, Bill Clinton had no trouble winning the nomination of the Democratic Party for a second term as president. Despite the continuous news coverage of various scandals, the public as a whole liked Bill and agreed with his policies. The Republican nominee was Senate majority leader Bob Dole of Kansas. Once again, Ross Perot ran on the third-party ticket, but he was considerably less successful than he had been four years earlier.

The press pitted Hillary against Dole's wife, Elizabeth "Liddy" Dole. Liddy, too, was a lawyer and businesswoman who had served as a cabinet secretary under two presidents and was head of the American Red Cross. The press continually compared the two women. In November, Bill Clinton beat Bob Dole 49.2 percent to 40.7 percent.

Soon after Bill's second inauguration, Chelsea graduated from high school. Her father was the main speaker. She had made the decision to go west to Stanford University in Palo Alto, California, for college. Both parents were dismayed at the long distance between Palo Alto and Washington, but they accepted her decision. They accompanied her to Stanford that fall and found it very hard to leave her there, alone. They knew they could no longer protect her from the news headlines that never seemed to stop. But Chelsea had learned at a young age that people could say terrible things about her parents, and she had learned to try to ignore them.

HILLARY THE WRITER

Whenever people attacked her, Hillary turned to activities more traditionally associated with first ladies. One of those activities was writing. She wrote a book called *It Takes a Village: And Other Lessons Children Teach Us*, published in 1996. It was a combination of her own experiences raising Chelsea, lessons she had learned while studying child development, and stories she had heard while working with families and children. She promoted the book in a tour of almost a dozen cities and made her own audio recording, which won a Grammy Award. Two years later, she wrote *Dear Socks, Dear Buddy: Kids' Letters to the First Pets*.

A very different book, *An Invitation to the White House: At Home with History*, came out in 2000. That same year, she wrote the foreword of an important book, *Saving America's Treasures*, which is about the important Save America's Treasures project that she and Bill helped launch. One important treasure that was saved as a result of the program was the original Star-Spangled Banner that flew over Fort Henry in the War of 1812.

A LAST STRAW

On June 30, 1998, independent counsel Kenneth Starr acknowledged to the public that he had failed to find any real evidence of wrongdoing on the parts of Hillary and Bill Clinton. Starr left Washington.

Republicans did not give up looking for a way to impeach Bill, however: "All that was needed was an offense that could be pinned on Clinton. But the supposedly big issues—Whitewater, Travelgate, Filegate, Vincent Foster's death, Mena drug trafficking [the false story that Bill was behind a drug smuggling scheme in Arkansas], even the wild-eyed lists of 'mysterious deaths'—failed to generate anything that approached convincing evidence."

But finally something did generate hard evidence. Her name was Monica Lewinsky.

CHAPTER SIX

Surviving Bill's Impeachment

WHEN HILLARY RODHAM MADE THE choice to marry Bill Clinton, she knew that she would probably always be fighting his tendency to get involved with other women. It was a facet of his character that she hated, but she accepted it because she loved him so much and knew that they would support each other in their ambitions.

Bill's presidential bid had started with tabloid articles about Gennifer Flowers. Despite the scandal, he was elected. He had been in office only a few months when Paula Jones's name surfaced. Hillary recommended that her husband not give Jones a large settlement of money in order to end the lawsuit. Hillary admitted that her advice was a mistake. Eventually, Bill was forced to testify about his actions with Jones, and the lies he told during his testimony led to his impeachment.

THE PRESENCE OF MONICA

In 1995 a young California native named Monica Lewinsky went to Washington as an unpaid intern to explore life in the nation's capital. She was lucky enough to get a job in the White House, where she met the president, Bill Clinton. They began what Bill later called an "inappropriate relationship." Lewinsky gained a paid position at the White House, and their relationship continued for more than a year, until superiors transferred her to the Pentagon. Even then, she and the president continued to talk on the phone.

Even during the impeachment proceedings, Hillary and Bill had to appear in public as if everything was normal.

At the Pentagon, Lewinsky met another employee, Linda Tripp, to whom she confessed her relationship with the president. Tripp secretly began to tape her and Lewinsky's phone conversations, during which she encouraged Lewinsky to talk about Bill. Before long Washingtonians began to whisper, "Did you hear about Bill and Monica?"

ENTER KENNETH STARR

In early January 1998, Linda Tripp informed Kenneth Starr, the independent counsel who had been investigating Whitewater, about the tapes she had made. Tripp most likely had made those tapes illegally, so Starr's staff arranged for Tripp to meet Lewinsky in public at a hotel near the Pentagon across the river in Virginia, where the laws were different. Tripp would wear a microphone that would record her conversation with Lewinsky. At the luncheon, everything was legal according to Virginia law. Starr learned enough for Lewinsky to be detained by the FBI. It was later reported that FBI agents threatened to send Lewinsky to jail if she did not cooperate and tell all.

The very next day, Bill Clinton testified about his relationship with Paula Jones to Jones's lawyers. He answered questions for six hours, thus making him the first sitting president ever to testify as the defendant in a lawsuit. Lewinsky's name was brought in to demonstrate that Bill made a habit of sexual harassment.

There wasn't anything illegal about the president having a relationship with an intern. But Starr sought to catch the president telling lies when he testified to Jones's lawyers. At that time Clinton had no idea that Monica Lewinsky had talked to anyone. And he flatly stated, "I have never had sexual relations with Monica Lewinsky."

Amazingly, not much of what was happening had reached the

public across the country. Then, on January 19, 1998, Bill and Lewinsky's relationship became public knowledge when an Internet news-and-gossip website reported that President Clinton had been having sexual encounters with an intern. The next day, the story appeared in the newspapers.

HILLARY BELIEVES

Bill quickly, and painfully, informed Hillary, before she could see the newspapers, about his relationship with Monica Lewinsky. He told her that the papers were going to report that he had asked Lewinsky to lie. He said that Lewinsky had misinterpreted his behavior, and that he was just trying to help her find her place in Washington.

This photo of President Clinton greeting Monica Lewinsky at a fund-raiser was shown on television and in newspapers many times.

Hillary accepted what Bill said. She later wrote,

> **" I will never truly understand what was going through my husband's mind that day. All I know is that Bill told his staff and our friends the same story he told me: that nothing improper went on. . . . In a better world, this sort of conversation between a husband and wife would be no one's business but our own. "**

Hillary had to deal with it. Knowing that the White House staff were looking to her for guidance on how they should react, she carried on with her regular tasks and appearances. Public opinion polls showed that President Clinton was still immensely popular with the American people.

A week later, Hillary appeared on NBC's *Today Show*. She blamed the Monica Lewinsky episode and the talk of impeachment on a "vast right-wing conspiracy." She said that the right-wing Republicans had been working against her husband since the day he announced his bid for president. Later, David Brock, one of the writers who had written vicious anti-Clinton articles that were published in right-wing periodicals, admitted that indeed there had been deliberate attempts to defame Clinton, and he apologized to Bill. He told the whole story of the conservative campaign to destroy Bill and his administration in his book *Blinded by the Right*.

The annual State of the Union address was coming up, and Bill did not want his own scandal to detract from it. So, the day before the address, he went on television. With Hillary standing behind him, he said to the American people,

> **I'm going to say this again: I did not have sexual relations with that woman, Miss Lewinsky. I never told anyone to lie, not a single time. Never. These allegations are false.**

THE GRAND JURY

Kenneth Starr convened a grand jury. Unlike a regular jury in a trial, a grand jury only determines whether there is enough evidence to charge, or indict, someone for a crime and bring him or her to trial. Also unlike a regular trial, a person testifying cannot have his or her lawyer present, nor is the press allowed to attend. Hoping to pick up tidbits of news, reporters hung around the site of the grand jury. Months were going by without any hard news, but there were frequent leaks of what went on in the grand jury room. Talk of impeachment was heating up.

In April, the judge in the Paula Jones case in Arkansas threw the case out. This made Bill look better, but it didn't stop Starr's investigation.

At the end of July, Starr granted Monica Lewinsky immunity. Whatever she said before the grand jury could not lead to her own prosecution. He was hoping to get her to admit that President Clinton had asked her to lie. But she did not. She only testified that she had had a sexual relationship with the president.

Then Bill himself agreed to testify before the grand jury, something that a U.S. president had never done. When that news broke, Bill confessed to Hillary that he had, in fact, lied to her. She wrote,

I was dumbfounded, heartbroken and outraged that I'd believed him at all.

Clearly, Hillary was very angry. She stopped defending Bill in public as she had done so often before. Columnist Margaret Carlson wrote, "The first lady may not be able to save the President the way she saved the candidate, but she surely will hurt him if she doesn't stand by him once again, and not like some potted plant."

Gradually, Hillary did begin to support Bill, once again. She later told reporter Mary Dejevsky, "There has been enormous pain, enormous anger, but I have been with him half my life and he is a very, very good man. We just have a deep connection that transcends whatever happens."

Many people speculated that Hillary would eventually divorce Bill. But those closest to her knew that the two of them had long been in love and made up two parts of a whole. They probably could not thrive without each other. Hillary wrote, "Although I was heartbroken and disappointed with Bill, my long hours alone made me admit to myself that I loved him. . . . As his wife, I wanted to wring Bill's neck. But he was not only my husband, he was also my President, and I thought that, in spite of everything, Bill led America and the world in a way that I continued to support."

The president testified before the grand jury by closed-circuit television from the White House on August 17. He was questioned for four hours. That same evening, he again went on television and spoke to the American people. He said that he had not told the truth to Hillary or to the American people: "Indeed, I did have a relationship with Miss Lewinsky that was not appropriate. In fact, it was wrong. It constituted a critical lapse in judgment and a personal failure on my part for which I am solely and completely responsible." But Bill went on to insist that he had not asked anyone to lie or to destroy evidence.

Bill continued, "Now, this matter is between me, the two people I love most—my wife and our daughter—and our God. I must put it right, and I am prepared to do whatever it takes to do so."

Chelsea was home from college, and she became the buffer between a very angry Hillary and an abject Bill as the family vacationed on Martha's Vineyard off Cape Cod. But they had to return to Washington, and Chelsea returned to Stanford. Her parents would have to find their own way back to talking to each other.

IMPEACHMENT

Hillary had worked on the impeachment of President Richard Nixon twenty-four years earlier, and she was certain that there were no constitutional grounds for her husband to be impeached. She knew, though, that continuing pressure from the media would eventually cause Congress to act, despite the fact that the public was opposed to the idea of impeaching the president.

On September 9, Kenneth Starr's people delivered his report and many boxes of documents to the House Judiciary Committee. Hillary wrote, "I've been told that the word *sex* (or some variation of it) appears 581 times in the 445-page report. Whitewater, the putative subject of Starr's probe, reportedly appears four times, to identify a figure, like the Whitewater Independent Counsel." It was the question of Whitewater that had set off the independent counsel in the first place, but he had never found anything to charge Bill or Hillary with.

That was an election year for Congress. Americans were angry with Bill, but they took Hillary to heart when she bravely campaigned for representatives and senators across the country. In the November election, the Democrats gained more seats in Congress than they had held before, thus reducing the Republican majority. The American people may not have approved of Bill's behavior, but they responded to Hillary's campaigning.

A month later, on December 11, the House Judiciary Committee approved four articles (itemized reasons) of impeachment, with a vote that was strictly Republicans against Democrats. Eight days later, the House of Representatives as a whole voted to impeach Bill Clinton. The articles had shrunk to two: perjury, or lying to a grand jury, and obstruction of justice. This was only the second time in American history that a president would be impeached.

Events then moved swiftly to the Senate, where Bill Clinton's trial started on January 7, with the chief justice of the Supreme Court presiding. It lasted a little over a month. When the final vote took place, the Republicans failed to get the number needed to convict. On February 12, 1999, the Senate acquitted Bill Clinton of the charges. He would hold on to the presidency. Bill and Hillary went on to serve out the remaining two years of his term in the White House.

WHAT NEXT?

During the 1998 campaign season, Hillary had spoken eight times in New York State in support of Chuck Schumer, who won New York's

Senate seat. Immediately after the election, the senior New York senator, Daniel Patrick Moynihan, announced that he would not run again. Hillary began to consider running for the position.

First she went on what she called a "listening tour." She traveled throughout the state of New York and talked to everyone who was willing to chat—in schools, factories, hospitals, housing projects, and other places. New Yorkers got a great chance to see Hillary up close, too.

Hillary could have gotten out of politics. She had many other opportunities open to her, such as running big businesses, hosting a TV show, writing newspaper columns, and running nonprofit foundations. But Hillary, who had never been elected to a government position but had been influential in policy making all her adult life, found herself intrigued by the idea of a Senate seat.

Joshua Green, writing many years later in *Atlantic Monthly*, described Hillary's decision-making process. He wrote that it "became easier—or at least victory seemed more probable—after Clinton found herself the unexpected beneficiary of glowing coverage during the Monica Lewinsky scandal, which broke early in 1998. As the wronged but dignified spouse, Clinton won public sympathy, and her favorability ratings soared. This must have been a disquieting experience. Clinton had always prided herself on her brains and talent, and now found herself rehabilitated largely for reasons owing nothing to them."

In June 1999, Hillary set up a committee to help her decide whether to run, which really meant that she had already decided. Hillary would move to New York and try to become the state's next U.S. senator.

CHAPTER SEVEN

Senator Clinton

L ONG BEFORE THE PUBLIC KNEW THAT she was interested in running for the Senate, Hillary and Bill discussed whether she should make a Senate bid or try to become Democrat Al Gore's vice presidential candidate. Staffers in the White House knew that there was, indeed, a plan by which the Clintons hoped eventually to switch places, with Hillary as president and Bill as the first "first gentleman."

Hillary and her staff debated whether she should run. Hillary later wrote,

> **One thing we talked about is euphemistically referred to as 'the spouse problem.' In my case, that was an understatement. It's always difficult to figure out the appropriate role for the wife or husband of a political candidate. My dilemma was unique. Some worried that Bill was still so popular in New York and such a towering political figure in America that I would never be able to establish an independent political voice. Others thought the controversy attached to him would overwhelm my message.**

Hillary Clinton during her campaign for the U.S. Senate seat in New York

During the deliberations about Hillary's bid for the Senate, she and Bill began speaking again. Slowly they were resuming their old footing as devoted and equal friends who valued each other's ideas.

In her book *Speaking of Hillary*, former congresswoman Patricia Schroeder of Colorado writes, "I chuckle when people ask why [Hillary] would run for Senate in New York. 'Doesn't she know [how] tough it will be?' they asked. Where have they been? Mars? Do they think she's been eating bon-bons and getting her hair done as first lady? I think she figures it's time for the family to support her emotionally and financially. She always puts her whole self into whatever she takes on. . . . I'm ready to stand up and shout, 'You go, girl!'"

Once Hillary made the decision to run, she and Bill had to become official residents of New York. They went shopping in the suburbs of New York City and found a beautiful old house in the small town of Chappaqua. Moving into it turned them into New York residents.

ON THE RUN

Before Hillary ran for the Senate, she had been involved in many campaigns, but these campaigns—at least since college—had been for her husband. This time, Hillary started out in a way that might have doomed her campaign. By inclination, she is not a glad-hander who can go into any crowd and feel comfortable, especially when she is talking about herself. At the beginning of her Senate campaign, Hillary hung back from crowds and did not mix with them. She turned down opportunities to have one-on-one interviews with the press, primarily because she was reluctant to discuss Bill and Monica Lewinsky.

If she had continued to hang back, Hillary probably could not have won the election. The voters didn't see her as a human being they could relate to. But Hillary knew what was wrong and made

Hillary and Bill became New Yorkers when they bought a home in the town of Chappaqua.

herself change. She talked up her own qualifications. She shook every hand that reached out toward her. She still never answered personal questions, but the voters seemed to accept that.

Traveling throughout the big state of New York, Hillary visited small towns, cities, and farms. She campaigned in restaurants, high school gyms, and churches in all sixty-two of the state's counties.

Every step of Hillary's campaign drew press coverage—and, as usual, criticism. Gradually, New Yorkers began to accept that she was serious. They began to listen to what she had to say instead of just viewing her as, in Hillary's own words, "a curiosity."

Many New Yorkers had encouraged Hillary to run for the Senate because they wanted a strong Democrat to stand up against Republican Rudy Giuliani, mayor of New York City. Giuliani would have been tough to beat, but about seven months before the election, he withdrew from the race due to a newly discovered cancer. Hillary's opponent was now Rick Lazio, a U.S. congressman. She and Lazio debated three times during the remaining campaign. During one debate, Lazio marched over to Hillary and demanded that she sign a pledge to limit campaign contributions. She refused, and the voters turned against Lazio for his aggressive action.

In November 2000, Hillary was elected New York's junior senator by a vote of 55 percent to 43 percent. Chelsea was able to cast her first official vote for her mother.

TAKING HER SEAT

On January 3, 2001, while she was still first lady and still living in the White House, Hillary took the oath of office for the Senate. It was her first oath as an elected official of the United States. She was one of a freshman class (first term) of eleven senators.

How do you fit in to a legislative body in which about half the members voted to convict your husband? It wasn't easy, but Hillary drew upon her characteristic determination to make it work. She did it by reaching "across the aisle"—working with Republicans on as much legislation as possible.

Hillary even went to Senator Robert Byrd of West Virginia and

CHELSEA GROWS UP

While Hillary was running for the Senate, Chelsea took on some of her mother's duties as White House hostess. In 2001 Chelsea graduated from Stanford University with a degree in history. She later earned a master's degree in international relations at Oxford University in England. Chelsea then went to work on Wall Street in New York City.

asked for his advice on how to be good at her new job. Byrd was the lawmaker who had squelched her health care bill. Byrd advised Hillary to be a "workhorse," not a "show horse."

All that Hillary had learned over her lifetime in politics informed her conduct as a senator. She understood how politics and government work, how to influence others to accomplish her goals, and perhaps most important, how to carry out the routine activities of committees in order to get bills passed into law. After working to be appointed to the Senate Armed Services Committee working with the Pentagon, she became fully involved in the committee's proceedings. Hillary had come a long way from her antiwar activities of many years before.

The Republicans found Hillary cooperative, willing, and a quick study. Gradually their opinions of her began to change. Years later, in the *Atlantic Monthly*, Joshua Green wrote that Hillary's accomplishments as senator were what qualified her to run for president, not her years in the White House. He wrote, "Clinton has emerged within the Senate as the unlikeliest of figures: she, not George W. Bush, has

Hillary Rodham Clinton being sworn in as the junior senator from New York on January 3, 2001

turned out to be a uniter, not a divider." Hillary was often able to bring Democrats and Republicans together so that progress could be made.

And what about Bill? After moving out of the White House, Bill formed the William J. Clinton Foundation. He began traveling the world, giving speeches, and collecting donations to use in fighting poverty, childhood obesity, climate change, and AIDS. To this day, Bill and Hillary talk on the phone several times a day. Bill likes to talk rather than using e-mail because he can tell by Hillary's voice how she is really feeling.

DEALING WITH TERRORISM

On September 11, 2001 (9/11), the city that Hillary had made her own was devastated when terrorists flew commercial airliners into the two huge skyscrapers of the World Trade Center. She and her onetime opponent, Mayor Giuliani, worked together to help New Yorkers heal.

Thirteen months later, the U.S. Senate voted to authorize President Bush to use military force in order to defend the national security of the United States against Iraq. Bush insisted that Iraq played a major role in the bombing of the World Trade Center and the resultant deaths of almost three thousand people. Senator Clinton voted with the majority. That vote would come back to haunt her in her bid for the presidency six years later—six years of ongoing war.

LOW-KEY ACHIEVEMENTS

Senators are supposed to work on behalf of the states they represent as well as working toward national goals. Hillary was proud of two achievements for New York State. The first was persuading the Senate Appropriations Committee to grant $20 billion in funds to aid New York City's recovery after 9/11. The second was preventing Niagara Falls Air Reserve Station from being shut down. That part of the state was economically depressed, and the station's closing would have sent it into further recession. These are the main accomplishments that sealed Hillary's reelection in 2006.

These issues were fairly low-key compared to the ones Hillary had tackled as first lady. However, Hillary knew that she would have to forego campaigning in the Senate for the big issues she favored,

New York governor George Pataki, New York City mayor Rudy Giuliani, and Senator Hillary Clinton after the bombing of the World Trade Center

especially universal health care. Public opinion about her personally could affect the vote on such issues. Instead, she concentrated her energy on smaller issues. Because of that, some people accused her of taking no risks. Hillary disagreed: "Everything I do carries political risk because nobody gets the scrutiny that I get. It's not like I have any margin for error whatsoever. I don't. Everybody else does, and I don't. And that's fine. That's just who I am, and that's what I live with."

Hillary received a lot more public scrutiny in June 2003 when her memoir, *Living History*, was published. An immediate best seller, it was bought by many people who hoped to learn the secrets of the Clintons' marriage. But as journalist Carl Bernstein writes in his biography of Hillary, *A Woman in Charge*, "She has always conspired to be better than conventional; *Living History* was meant to demonstrate that. But judged against the facts, it underlines how she has often chosen to obfuscate, omit, and avoid. It is an understatement by now that she has been known to apprehend truths about herself and the events of her life that others do not exactly share. *Living History* is an example of that."

Joshua Green, who often wrote about Hillary, noted, "The biggest surprise for me . . . was discovering what a chauvinistic institution the Senate still is, and what women have to endure and overcome to be taken seriously there. Until a few years ago, they were required to wear lipstick and skirts. The fact that Clinton could flourish despite this environment gives you a sense of her formidable political skills." There were always reminders that Hillary was former president Clinton's wife. Until Senator Barack Obama was running for president, Hillary was the only senator who was always accompanied by a Secret Service detail, though the men and women protecting her were rarely visible to someone not looking for them.

In 2006 Hillary was up for reelection. Six years had passed. She dared not let New Yorkers know that she was interested in the presidency, or they might not reelect her. She beat Republican opponent John Spencer, a former mayor of Yonkers, with 67 percent of the vote. Now she was New York's senator as well as a presidential candidate. While she was campaigning for New Yorkers, however, she neglected to do what presidential candidates must do: get to know voters in Iowa. This mistake would hurt her when the people of Iowa voted on her presidential candidacy in early 2008.

CHAPTER EIGHT

Eighteen Million Cracks in the Glass Ceiling

I N 2003 MAX J. SKIDMORE, A POLITICAL science professor at the University of Missouri, wrote, "Sometime early in the twenty-first century, the United States will swear into office a new president who, for the first time in the country's history—a history of more than two centuries—will be a woman. She will be a seasoned politician. She will likely command wide support. She will have demonstrated the success of an arduous struggle to overcome a bias against women that long permeated an entire culture; a bias so strong that it included even figures as enlightened as Thomas Jefferson." Skidmore added that Jefferson and most other men believed that if a woman were to mix easily with men, such as in the political arena, people would rightly question who the father of her children was.

Shortly after Skidmore wrote that, political enthusiasts were talking about the possibility that Hillary Rodham Clinton would be the first woman president of the United States.

Mark Penn, the pollster who worked for the Clintons, tested public opinion in 2003 to see if Hillary should run for president. The result was positive, but Hillary was not yet interested in running. A poll two years later could be summed up by one comment: "If Hillary runs, Hillary wins—simple as that."

Hillary's supporters made the following comments:

" Senator Clinton will be the first woman to be a competitive Democratic contender and she will take off like a rocket.

Hillary campaigning for the Democratic nomination for president, with Bill and Chelsea beside her

> **Hillary would have to screw up in a big way to blow her current advantage over the rest of the field, which is unlikely.**

> **Strong favorite if she runs—nearly perfect pitch in the Senate thus far.**

Republican poll respondents who thought Hillary couldn't win consistently said that she was too liberal for the country as a whole. Others were certain that the country was not yet ready for a woman president, especially one who was seen as "strident and shrill."

One unidentified respondent said,

> **I don't think she can win a general election. But she should run because she will make every other candidate better. If one of them beats her, he or she will be a much stronger general election candidate. If no one can beat her [in the primaries], then no one else should be the nominee.**

A WOMAN FOR PRESIDENT

Hillary Clinton is the third woman in U.S. history to compete in the major party presidential primaries. Margaret Chase Smith, a Republican from Maine, got twenty-seven delegate votes in the 1964 campaign, which led to Barry Goldwater's nomination. Senator Smith was the first person in Congress with the spine to stand up to Senator Joseph McCarthy, who blindly and wrongly accused people of being communists. She made the Republicans nervous when she entered the New Hampshire primary. But she seemed unsure of exactly how a woman was supposed to run for president, and soon she resorted to passing out muffins on her campaign stops.

Eight years later, Shirley Chisholm, a Democrat of New York, won 152 delegates, making her the first major party black candidate, as well as the first female Democratic candidate. Chisholm fought the good fight, but none of the male candidates ever considered her a serious threat.

STARTING ON THE TRAIL

Hillary's senatorial campaign didn't stop the press from talking about her as a presidential candidate, an idea that was controversial from day one. *New York Times* writer Anne Kornblut, who called Hillary "the woman in the pantsuit," wrote, "Although polls show most Americans say they are willing to vote for a woman—more than 90 percent of those surveyed would do so for the right candidate—far fewer, about 55 percent, believe the country as a whole is ready for a female president.

Broadly, the data suggest that there is a lingering awkwardness toward women at the tip-top of political power, both on screen and off." Hillary was determined to overcome that awkwardness.

Women have held the top political position in other countries. In 2005, for example, Angela Merkel was elected chancellor of Germany and Ellen Johnson Sirleaf was elected president of Liberia. The next year, Michelle Bachelet was elected president of Chile.

IT STARTED IN IOWA, JANUARY 3, 2008

As the Iowa caucuses—the first test of a presidential campaign's strength—neared, Iowans marveled at the efficiency of Barack Obama's campaign and questioned why Hillary's campaign seemed disorganized. Hillary tried to get her campaign to attack Obama, but it was too late.

In her Iowa speech, Hillary said,

> **We used to say in the White House that if a place is too dangerous, too small or too poor, send the first lady.**

As an example, she said that in 1996, snipers had shot at her at an airport in Bosnia. She had to duck while running from their airplane to cover. The anecdote made Hillary sound as if she really could be the nation's commander in chief. However, films of the actual event in Bosnia showed a child greeting Hillary on the runway with flowers, with no gunfire anywhere.

Hillary finished third in Iowa, after Barack Obama and John Edwards. Her campaign workers were stunned. They had assumed that she could not lose. They also had assumed that fewer than 100,000 voters would turn out at the caucuses on a snowy Iowa evening. Instead, Obama had inspired and registered many young voters, and more than 250,000 people turned out. About one-fourth of the voters at the caucuses were under the age of twenty-five. Only 5 percent of the young voters opted for Hillary. Astonishingly, she earned fewer votes from women than Obama did. She was going to have to reconfigure her campaign.

However, just before the primary vote in New Hampshire, a week later, a woman in a small circle around Hillary asked, "How do you keep so upbeat and so wonderful?" In replying, Hillary's voice cracked and her eyes teared up, just briefly. Hillary was appalled, certain that she had just lost the race. She thought the American people would vote for a woman only if she always appeared strong and never seemed vulnerable.

But the women of New Hampshire came out for Hillary in large numbers, and they gave Hillary her first win.

SUPER TUESDAY

Seven other primaries and caucuses were held during the next few weeks. Success moved back and forth between Obama and Hillary. Hillary supporters didn't know what to do. With all the flip-flopping, would-be donors were not sending in the money she needed to continue her campaign. She loaned her campaign $5 million of her own money, the first of several loans she would make. When her supporters learned what she had done, money poured in, especially from women.

DELEGATES
AND SUPER DELEGATES

The primary elections in most states are the means for candidates to win their delegates—people who are committed to vote for them—at the political parties' national conventions, where they nominate their candidate for president. Most states allot all their delegates to the person who wins the most votes, though a few split them up among the various candidates. Super delegates exist only in the Democratic Party. They are generally people of national importance to the party who commit to a candidate on their own decision. In the 2008 primaries, most super delegates withheld their opinions until after the primary contests between Hillary and Obama had ended.

Hillary predicted that the primary races would be over on February 5, which was called Super Tuesday. Primaries were being held in more states in one day than ever before. Hillary was certain that the wins she anticipated on that day would take her over the top.

On Super Tuesday Hillary did indeed win some major states, such as New York, New Jersey, and California. But her campaign managers hadn't anticipated that all the small states—states her campaign had mostly ignored—would add up to give Obama more delegates than Hillary won in her few big states.

During the remaining primaries, Obama won a string of thirteen primaries and nine caucuses. That left Hillary with only one way to win the nomination: she had to persuade more of the super delegates that she was the right candidate. But it was too late. One by one, super delegates began to announce that they would be voting for Barack Obama. They thought he had a better chance of winning the votes of independents. They also didn't want to be seen voting against an African American.

Hillary accused Obama of having nothing to campaign on except one speech, the one he made in Illinois in which he said the United States should not go to war against Iraq. Obama retorted, what good is all her experience if she voted so badly on the one big vote (on the war with Iraq) she made in the Senate? Throughout the campaign Hillary kept insisting that she had not voted to wage a full-blown war, just to authorize the president to go to war if he chose to. She refused to repudiate that vote. Many Americans, who had long since decided that the war with Iraq was wrong, held that stubbornness against her.

BRINGING IN BILL

Many voters liked the idea of voting for Hillary because they had liked Bill as president. Hillary had to separate herself from Clintonism, however. She had to let the public know that she would be a different Clinton, not a rerun of Bill's eight years. One commentator wrote,

> **Clinton's team often seems perplexed by a political quandary unlike any that has come before: how to exploit all the good will that Democrats have for Bill Clinton without allowing Hillary Clinton to become a constant reminder of the things they didn't like about his presidency.**

Bill thought he was helping his wife, but often his presence just reminded people of all the Clinton scandals. He wanted to appear for her in South Carolina, where more than half the voters were black. He thought he could dampen some of the enthusiasm for Obama. Instead, he lost a lot of black votes by continually referring to Obama as merely "the black candidate" and comparing him to Jesse Jackson, who had, indeed, been "the black candidate" in 1984 and 1988. People accused Bill of bringing race into the contest instead of qualifications.

As the primaries ground on, the campaign deployed Bill Clinton more strategically (and, perhaps, more effectively) in the kinds of smaller towns presidents never visit—forty-seven stops in Pennsylvania, thirty-nine in Indiana, fifty in North Carolina—where he campaigned for Hillary in largely white, working-class areas but, poignantly for a man once dubbed the nation's "first black president," not in African-American ones.

Some of Hillary's campaign people wanted her to remind audiences of Obama's "otherness"—that because of his mixed-race parentage and childhood spent in Indonesia, he was different from them. But Hillary refused to play along with that kind of negative campaigning. She also refused to take advantage of terrible, apparently anti-American remarks made by the minister of Obama's Chicago church.

As Hillary spoke in Indiana the night before the final primary, Bill and Chelsea stood behind her. Hillary said, "No matter what happens, I will work for the nominee of the Democratic Party because we must win in November."

Hillary won the contest in Indiana, but Obama's win in North Carolina on the same day guaranteed him the number of delegates he needed. On NBC, Tim Russert pronounced, "We now

THE GLASS CEILING

Ending her concession speech on June 7, 2008, Hillary said, "Although we weren't able to shatter that highest, hardest glass ceiling this time, thanks to you, it's got about 18 million cracks in it. And the light is shining through like never before, filling us all with the hope and the sure knowledge that the path will be a little easier next time." She was referring to the metaphor that women have been unable to break through the barriers against their taking up high-level positions in business and government. The term *glass ceiling* has been in use since it first appeared in a business journal in 1984.

know who the Democratic nominee is going to be, and no one is going to dispute it."

CARRYING ON, REGARDLESS

Hillary refused to acknowledge that she had lost. She kept hoping that enough super delegates would come out in her favor to change the result. But that didn't happen. Throughout May, she won several more states, including a huge blowout in West Virginia. In fact, she won the last ten contests, but she never overcame Obama's lead.

On June 7, 2008, Hillary held a huge gathering of her supporters at the National Building Museum in Washington, D.C. She finally conceded that Obama had won the nomination. She thanked all her supporters and donors and then concluded that she hoped all of them would join her in the effort to get Barack Obama elected president.

On June 28 Hillary and Obama met at Unity, New Hampshire, to shake hands and to agree to work together. The tiny town had split right down the middle in the Democratic primary. Each candidate had received 107 votes.

Hillary supporters promptly brought up the possibility that Obama would select her as his vice presidential candidate. But she privately told him not to even bring it up unless he was totally serious. The speculation ended when, back in Springfield, Illinois, where his campaign began, Obama announced that his selection for vice president was Joe Biden, an expert on world affairs and senator from Delaware since 1973.

AT THE CONVENTION

On August 26 Senator Clinton spoke at the National Democratic Convention. In the first sentence of her speech she called herself "a proud supporter of Barack Obama." The huge audience raised the roof with celebration and relief. Hillary was finally on the side of the man they were about to nominate as president.

She went on to say, "My friends, it is time to take back the country we love. Whether you voted for me, or voted for Barack, the time is now to unite as a single party with a single purpose. We are on the same team, and none of us can sit on the sidelines. This is a fight for the future. And it's a fight we must win." She described the struggle to give women the vote and added, "My mother was born before women could vote. But in this election my daughter got to vote for her mother for president."

The next day, about half the state delegations had been called on in alphabetical order to announce their nominee for president.

Democratic nominee Barack Obama and Hillary Clinton met in Unity,
New Hampshire, to demonstrate their unity in the 2008 presidential campaign.

Obama was ahead in the delegate count, 1,549.5 to 341.5. New Mexico yielded to Illinois, which had passed earlier. Illinois then yielded to New York. Hillary walked into the convention hall surrounded by the other New York delegates. She took the microphone and made a motion that the delegates unanimously support Barack Obama "with eyes firmly fixed on the future." The convention suspended the roll call and announced Obama as the party's nominee for president.

Just before the Republican National Convention, nominee John McCain surprised everyone by naming Sarah Palin, governor of Alaska, as his vice presidential running mate. Perhaps he hoped that having a woman on the ticket would draw female voters who were upset that Hillary had lost.

WHY DIDN'T HILLARY WIN?

Perhaps Hillary's main mistake was misjudging the mood of the country. She emphasized her experience and preparedness, while the country was looking for change. Probably another mistake was in building her campaign team with people who were loyal to her instead of experienced campaigners who knew how to win. In the same way, she looked to experienced donors of campaign funds instead of trying to draw in new ones, as Obama had, in huge numbers.

Even before she lost the nomination, people were talking about Hillary's bitterness at the "sexist" treatment she had received. For example, reporters would comment about the pearls she often wore or the cosmetic frosting that had been added to her hair. People argued that reporters did not make such comments about male candidates. "Sexism is part of our culture," Hillary said to Fox News.

In her book *Why Women Should Rule the World*, which was published before the presidential primaries were finished, Dee Dee Myers writes, "What about Hillary Clinton, the most successful female presidential candidate in American history? It seems that not just her policies but often her approach also tilt masculine. And that may help explain why voters have yet to fall in love with her: In a world where people have different expectations for women, she pays a price for showing us her steel spine more often than her soft heart."

It is difficult to determine just what role sexism played in Hillary's loss, but her Senate vote on the war in Iraq was a major disadvantage. Unlike candidate John Edwards, Hillary never said that her vote had been a mistake. Although Barack Obama was not in the Senate when that critical vote was taken, he had spoken out against the war.

THE GENERAL ELECTION

Although the press did not pay a lot of attention, Hillary kept her promise to work for Barack Obama's presidency. She appeared at more than two hundred rallies and fund-raisers for Obama and other Democratic candidates across the country. Not all the fund-raisers were for other candidates; she still had to pay off her massive $25.2 million debt from her own campaign. She succeeded in paying off most of this debt during the general election campaign, but she had yet to recuperate the $13 million she had personally loaned her campaign.

When Republican nominee John McCain lost the election in November, his supporters said that he had lost the election by not campaigning during the Obama-Clinton drama and by choosing Sarah Palin as his running mate. Only one in five Hillary voters switched their allegiance to McCain. Were these voters protesting her losing the Democratic primary? Did they refuse to vote for an African-American candidate?

The answer is unknown. Perhaps in the dark of night, Hillary ponders what happened to her campaign. But if so, she is too busy to think about it in the daytime. While President Obama did not make Hillary his running mate, he chose her for what may be the most important job outside the White House

CHAPTER NINE

Madame Secretary

I N THE INTRODUCTION TO HER 2003 BOOK, *Living History*, Hillary wrote that as first lady, she had learned "the importance of America's engagement with the rest of the world, and I developed relationships with foreign leaders and an understanding of foreign cultures that come in handy today." She could not have known just how handy that experience would become in 2009.

Hillary had returned to the Senate after finally acknowledging that Obama was the Democratic nominee. But she kept her promise to campaign for him, and on November 4, 2008, Barack Obama was elected president, the first African American to hold the office.

Karen Tumulty of *Time* magazine asked what would become of Hillary after the election. There were many suggestions: become governor of New York, try to become Senate majority leader, hold out for an appointment to the Supreme Court. But Hillary herself said that she was most interested in going back to the effort that had failed when she was in the White House with Bill, getting health care for everyone:

> **I'm interested in standing on the South Lawn of the White House and seeing President Obama signing into law quality, affordable health care for everybody, and voting in a big majority for clean, renewable energy and smarter economic policies.**

President-elect Barack Obama nominated Hillary as his secretary of state in a Chicago press conference.

But where would Hillary fit in this picture? Journalist Josh Green had written earlier, "As an admiring senator put it to me, 'Hillary Clinton is everyone's secret choice for majority leader.' It's a line you hear often on Capitol Hill, and it has two possible meanings. For some it's polite code for 'Lord, I hope she doesn't run for president.' But for others—I'd venture to say the majority—it is a compliment genuinely felt, an acknowledgment that she has satisfied the lions of the Senate and, should she wish to, might one day rank among them."

But it was very unlikely that Hillary would become Senate majority leader. She wasn't even the senior senator from New York—Chuck Schumer was ahead of her in rank. And there were many other senators who would be vying for the position. Some commentators, however, thought that Hillary would not be happy back in the Senate. They felt she needed a bigger platform because she was the biggest name in Washington other than President Obama.

SENDING OUT HER NAME

Hillary flew to Chicago to meet with president-elect Obama. People began to spread rumors that Obama might be considering her for secretary of state. Some people were puzzled that Hillary would consider the position because it would mean that, as part of the Obama administration, she would not be free to campaign for the presidency again in 2012. Others thought the position would be an excellent choice, and it would certainly be a bigger platform for her. The U.S. Department of State, which she would head, is the oldest and, many say, most important of the government departments. It has thousands of employees doing diplomatic work around the globe.

Since Obama was called No Drama Obama throughout his

campaign, people wondered why he would consider appointing Hillary as his secretary of state. Drama always seemed to surround the Clintons. But President Obama wanted to keep talent of all kinds around him. He did not want to hear only his own views reflected at him.

During the primary election campaign, Hillary's main criticism of Obama's foreign policy ideas was that he was willing to talk with certain leaders and dictators without setting some preconditions for the talks. She and others thought that was naïve. She felt the time and reputation of the president should not be wasted on discussions that might never lead to a diplomatic success.

Bill was also regarded as a stumbling block. He had long denied public access to the list of foreign leaders who had contributed to his presidential library and to his huge international charitable organization, Clinton Global Initiative. But in order for his wife to accept the position of secretary of state, he had to agree to release the names. After the public held its breath for several days, Bill agreed to do so, and he also promised that the White House could scrutinize any new commitments he made or contributions he received to be sure they did not conflict with Hillary's policy making. He also agreed not to participate in the day-to-day management of his foundation while his wife served as secretary of state.

Once the news about Hillary's nomination was out, she began meeting with people to get up to speed on the job of secretary of state. She received policy briefings almost every day.

Condoleezza Rice, President George W. Bush's secretary of state, invited Hillary to dinner at her apartment. In a casual, comfortable setting, they discussed the day-to-day life of a secretary of state and how to manage the huge bureaucracy of the State Department. Rice said, "Hillary Clinton is somebody of intelligence, and she'll do a great job. She also has what's most important to being secretary of state, and that is that you love this country and you represent it from a basis of faith in its values."

HILLARY'S CONFIRMATION

In the Senate, Hillary had always understood the details of all the bills being discussed. She often knew more than any other senator except those sponsoring a bill. In exactly the same way, she testified before the Senate Foreign Relations Committee in order to be confirmed in her new position of secretary of state. She knew the countries, the leaders, and the problems she would face in coming years. Even her enemies acknowledged that it was an impressive performance. Harking back to her speech in Beijing, China, Hillary also testified about her perpetual concern about women. She said, "Of particular concern to me is the plight of women and girls, who comprise the majority of the world's unhealthy, unschooled, unfed and unpaid. If half of the world's population remains vulnerable to economic, political, legal, and social marginalization, our hope of advancing democracy and prosperity will remain in serious jeopardy." She added that she views these issues as "central to our foreign policy, not as adjunct or in any way lesser."

On January 15, 2009, the Senate Foreign Relations Committee approved Hillary as secretary of state by a 16-to-1 vote. The only no vote was a Republican from Louisiana. On the day after President Obama's January 20 inauguration, the Senate confirmed Hillary as secretary of state.

Within an hour of the confirmation, Hillary was sworn in to the position in a private ceremony in her own Senate office. She used her father's Bible to take the oath of office. An old friend of Hillary's, federal court of appeals judge Kathryn Oberly, administered the oath.

Hillary Clinton, accompanied by senior New York senator Chuck Schumer, taking her seat at her confirmation hearing before the Senate Foreign Relations Committee

One day later, she was sworn in again, this time publicly. That second ceremony was carried out by Vice President Joe Biden. Both she and Biden acknowledged that they found themselves in strange jobs, ones they had not anticipated.

WHAT HILLARY OFFERS

Often, secretaries of state are individuals who have stood apart from the fray of politics. They have no base of supporters backing them. Hillary, however, has millions of people wishing the best for her. When she was chosen as secretary of state, she brought a lot of other people along with her. One of those supporters was General David Petraeus, who was in charge of the war in Afghanistan and Iraq. He said that Secretary of State Clinton really understood the military. He knew this from seeing her in action on the Senate Armed Services Committee.

THE STATE DEPARTMENT

The U.S. Department of State is the oldest of the departments that make up the executive branch of the federal government. Congress established it as the Department of Foreign Affairs in 1789. Thomas Jefferson was the first secretary of state. The first female secretary was Madeleine Albright, named by President Bill Clinton in 1996.

Many State Department employees belong to the U.S. Foreign Service and work for the United States in more than 250 locations around the world. Some Foreign Service diplomats make it all the way to the top and serve as ambassadors to other countries. Other ambassadors are political appointees.

You may have heard the puzzling term *Foggy Bottom*. It refers to the State Department, which is headquartered in the Harry S. Truman Building in an area of Washington, D.C., that is low lying and apt to collect fog. About 5,000 employees work at Foggy Bottom, while about 11,000 people are in the Foreign Service.

Hillary also brings to the job a distinctive background and unique skills. As first lady, she traveled the world for eight years and visited more than eighty countries. She not only met with foreign leaders but also visited villages, clinics, and remote areas that rarely appear on a president's itinerary. Former secretary of state Warren Christopher called Hillary a "naturally gifted diplomat."

Hillary promised a return to a foreign policy based on "principles and pragmatism, not rigid ideology; on facts and evidence, not emotion or prejudice." She offered a State Department that would "be firing on all cylinders to provide forward-looking, sustained diplomacy in every part of the world."

Within days, working with the president, Hillary appointed special envoys to work with the Middle East and another to deal with Afghanistan and Pakistan. Then, surprising most of the public, she also named a special envoy to work with the rest of the world on climate change. For her, diplomatic conversations would not just include wars and human rights. She would also talk with other countries about taking care of the planet.

When Obama announced that he had chosen Hillary as his secretary of state, the economy of the nation and the world was falling apart. Some people said that Obama would have to concentrate so completely on business that he was putting the rest of the world in her care. That wasn't really so, but as Hillary said, "America cannot solve these crises without the world. And the world cannot solve them without America."

And Hillary does not work alone. President Obama made her part of a team of national security advisers, and she works directly with the White House. When she thought she was going to be the presidential candidate, Hillary had talked to General Jim Jones, with whom she already had a good relationship, about serving as her secretary of defense. Later, Obama chose Jones as his national security adviser. The team also included Vice President Joe Biden, the secretary of defense, the attorney general (who heads the U.S. Department of Justice), and the secretary of homeland security. In a break with tradition, Obama also included the U.S, ambassador to the United Nations.

Among the world situations Secretary Clinton faces is how to deal with China. She is adamant about protecting human rights in any nation, but her position may be weakened since China has loaned the

United States huge amounts of money. As Hillary said, "How do you get tough with your banker?"

Before his inauguration, president-elect Obama announced that he hoped to turn the civil service (professional government employees) for the state department once again into a worthy career track for a young person. During recent years, career civil servants have become discouraged because all good foreign jobs have gone to political choices. It will be Hillary's job to see that this change is made. When she showed up for work on January 22, the entire staff of the State Department greeted her with cheers and applause. They hope that Hillary and President Obama will restore the State Department to its former stature, when it played the central role in American diplomacy.

In February 2009 Hillary made her first official visit abroad as secretary of state. Instead of going to Europe as secretaries usually have in the past, she went to the Far East—Japan, Indonesia, and China. In her talks with officials and citizens in those countries, she made it clear that she wouldn't be focusing on just the issues of traditional foreign relations. Instead, she was going to deal with climate change, energy, poverty, and, returning to the 1994 speech she made in Beijing, the advancement of women.

Hillary spent as much time with the public as she did with government officials. She appeared on TV shows, at colleges, and in restaurants. She said,

Showing up is not all of life, but it counts for a lot and especially when you are the most powerful country in the world, if you're not paying attention, people are going to feel like somehow they're not important to you.

HILLARY CLINTON

Secretary of State Hillary Clinton with Indonesian children on her
first visit abroad as head of the United States diplomatic efforts

The girl from Park Ridge, Illinois, had moved from the small stage
of running for high school office, through the White House, and on to
a world stage. When she speaks with foreign leaders, Hillary Rodham
Clinton speaks with the voice of the American people.

TIMELINE

1947 — Born in Chicago, Illinois

1965 — Graduates from Maine South High School; enters Wellesley College

1968 — Joins the Democratic Party

1969 — Graduates from Wellesley College; enters Yale Law School

1971 — Meets Bill Clinton; studies problems of migrant workers

1973 — Receives law degree and graduates with honors

1975 — Marries Bill Clinton

1976 — Joins Rose Law Firm in Little Rock, Arkansas

1978 — Becomes first lady of Arkansas when Bill is elected governor

1979 — Becomes first female full partner in Rose Law Firm

1980 — Daughter Chelsea Victoria is born; Bill fails to be reelected governor

1982	Begins to use last name of Clinton; becomes first lady of Arkansas again when Bill is elected governor, a position he holds for next ten years
1993	Becomes first lady when Bill is sworn in as forty-second president; he quickly names her to head the health care task force
1996	Bill is reelected president
1999	Bill Clinton is acquitted of impeachment charges
2000	Decides to run for the Senate and buys home in Chappaqua, New York
2001	Takes seat as U.S. senator from New York
2006	Reelected to the Senate while contemplating run for the presidency
2007	Announces intention to run for the presidency
2008	Barack Obama earns sufficient delegates to win the Democratic nomination
	Named secretary of state by president-elect Barack Obama
2009	Confirmed by the Senate as secretary of state

SOURCE NOTES

Boxed quotes unless otherwise noted

CHAPTER 1

p. 9, par. 4, Gail Sheehy, *Hillary's Choice* (New York: Random House, 1999), p. 24.

CHAPTER 2

p. 18, par. 2, Hillary Rodham Clinton, *Living History* (New York: Scribner, 2003), p. 37.

p. 21, par. 2, Clinton, *Living History*, p. 41.

p. 21, par. 4, Hillary D. Rodham , Wellesley College 1969 Student Commencement Speech, www.wellesley.edu/PublicAffairs/Commencement/1969/053169hillary.html

p. 22, par. 1, Clinton, *Living History*, p. 42.

p. 23, par. 3, Gwen Ifill, "Man in the News: William Jefferson Clinton Biography of a Candidate; Tenacity and Change in a Son of the South" *New York Times*, July 16, 1992.

p. 23, par. 4, *Living History*, pp. 53-54.

p. 23, par. 4, Bill Clinton, *My Life* (New York: Alfred A. Knopf, 2004), p. 184.

CHAPTER 3

p. 32, par. 1, Joshua Green, "Take Two: Hillary's Choice," *Atlantic Monthly*, November 2006.

p. 32, par. 3, Quoted in Sheehy, *Hillary's Choice*, as from *The New Straits Times*, September 19, 1999.

p. 34, par. 1, Clinton, *My Life*, p. 341.

p. 34, par. 3, Ifill, "Man in the News."

CHAPTER 4

p. 37, par. 1, Bill Clinton for President announcement speech, October 3, 1991, www.4president.org

p. 37, par. 3, Clinton, *Living History*, p. 111.

p. 38, par. 2, Clinton, *Living History*, p. 107.

p. 38, par. 4, Sheehy, *Hillary's Choice*, p. 200.

p. 39, par. 2, Ifill, "Trapped in a Spotlight, Hillary Clinton Uses It," *New York Times*, Feb. 3, 1992.

p. 41, par. 1, Amy Wilentz, "Yellow Pantsuit" in *Thirty Ways of Looking at Hillary: Reflections by Women Writers*, edited by Susan Morrison (New York: HarperCollins, 2008), p. 3.

p. 41, par. 2, Maureen Dowd, "The 1992 Campaign: Candidate's Wife; Hillary Clinton as Aspiring First Lady: Role Model, or a 'Hall Monitor' Type?" *New York Times*, May 18, 1992.

pp. 41-42, www.wellesley.edu/PublicAffairs/Commencement/1992/speecheshrc.html

p. 42, par. 2 and 3, Joyce Purnick, "Editorial Notebook: Let Hillary Be Hillary," *New York Times*, July 15, 1992.

CHAPTER 5

p. 45, par. 3, Robert Pear, "Settling In: First Lady," *New York Times*, January 22, 1993.

p. 48, par. 1, Quoted in Green, "Take Two."

p. 49, par. 1, Quoted in Green, "Take Two."

p. 49, par. 4, Jonathan Alter, "The Clintons," *Newsweek*, Jan 5, 2009.

p. 52, par. 3, Clinton, *Living History*, p. 297.

p. 53, par. 1, Paul Kengor, *God and Hillary Clinton: A Spiritual Life* (New York: HarperCollins, 2007), p. 128.

p. 55, par. 2, Hillary Clinton "Women's Rights are Human Rights," Beijing, China, September 5, 1995, www.famousquotes.me.uk/speeches/Hillary-Clinton/

p. 57, par. 4, Consortiumnews.com editorial, December 29, 1998.

CHAPTER 6

p. 60, par. 4, "Deposition in the Jones sexual harassment lawsuit," Washingtonpost.com, January 17, 1998.

p. 62, par. 1, Clinton, *Living History*, p. 441.

p. 63, par. 1, President Bill Clinton on television, January 26, 1998, video on washingtonpost.com/wp-srv/politics/special/clinton/stories/deny012798.htm

p. 64, par. 1, Clinton, *Living History*, p. 466.

p. 64, par. 2, Margaret Carlson, "The Shadow of Her Smile," *Time*, September 21, 1998.

p. 64, par. 3, Mary Dejevsky, "'I Still Love Bill Despite His Weaknesses,' Says Hillary," *The Independent*, August 2, 1999.

p. 64, par. 4, Clinton, *Living History*, p. 471.

p. 65-66, Clinton, *Living History*, p. 475.

p. 67, par. 4, Green, "Take Two."

CHAPTER 7

p. 69, par. 1, Described in Christopher Anderson, *The American Evita: Hillary Clinton's Path to Power* (New York: William Morrow, 2004), p. 4.

p. 69, par. 2, Clinton, *Living History*, p. 500.

p. 70, par. 2, Quoted in Susan K. Flinn, ed., *Speaking of Hillary* (Ashland, OR: White Cloud Press, 2000), p. 311.

p. 73, par. 4, Green, "Take Two."

p. 73-74, Joshua Green in an interview with Abigail Cutler, "Candidate Hillary," Atlantic Online, www.theatlantic.com, October 16, 2006.

p. 76, par. 1, Quoted by Green in Cutler interview, "Candidate Hillary."

p. 77, par. 1, Carl Bernstein, *A Woman in Charge* (New York: Alfred A. Knopf, 2007), p. 552.

p. 77, par. 2, Green in Cutler interview, "Candidate Hillary."

CHAPTER 8

p. 79, par. 1, Max J. Skidmore, "Breaking the Final Glass Ceiling: When (Not IF) a Woman Becomes President," in Robert P. Watson and Ann Gordon, editors, *Anticipating Madame President*, Boulder, CO: Lynne Rienner Publishers, 2003, p. 21.

pp. 79-80, Quoted in James A. Barnes and Peter Bell, poll reported in *Atlantic Monthly*, July/August 2005.

pp. 81-82, Anne Kornblut, "The Ascent of a Woman," *New York Times*, June 11, 2006.

p. 82, par. 4, R. J. Eskow, "How Will Hillary's Bosnia 'Whopper' Play in the Media?" www.huffingtonpost.com, March 21, 2008.

p. 83, par. 2, Quoted in Michiko Kakutani, "Candidate Clinton Scrutinized by Women," *New York Times*, January 15, 2008.

p. 85, par. 3, Matt Bai, "The Clinton Referendum," *New York Times Magazine*, December 23, 2007.

p. 86, par. 2, Bill Clinton was first publicly called this in an article by Toni Morrison, "Clinton as the First Black President," *The New Yorker*, October 1998.

p. 86, par. 4, abcnews.com, May 6, 2008.

p. 87, par. 1, "Hillary Clinton Endorses Barack Obama," *New York Times*, June 7, 2008.

p. 88, par. 5-6, "Hillary Clinton Democratic Convention Speech," www.huffingtonpost.com, August 26, 2008.

p. 89, par. 1, Elizabeth Benjamin, "Hillary's Acclamation Moment," www.nydailynews.com, August 27, 2008.

p. 90, par. 4, Dee Dee Myers, *Why Women Should Rule the World* (New York: HarperCollins, 2008), p. 125.

CHAPTER 9

p. 93, par. 1, Clinton, *Living History*, Page xiv.

p. 93, par. 3, Karen Tumulty, "The Once and Future Hillary," *Time*, November 17, 2007, pp 80-81.

p. 94, par. 1, Green, 'Take Two."

p. 96, par. 3, Domenico Montanaro, in "First Read" on msnbc.com, December 8, 2008.

p. 97-98, "Transcript of Clinton Confirmation Hearing," www.npr.org, January 13, 2009.

p. 99, par. 4, Quoted in "Secretary Christopher on Secretary Clinton," *Los Angeles Times*, November 21, 2009.

p. 99-100, *New York Times editorial*, January 13, 2009.

p. 100, par. 3, Quoted in "Secretary of State Hillary Clinton," www.time.com, December 2, 2008.

p. 101, par. 2, Quoted in Michael Goodwin, "In China, Hillary Clinton Plays a Weak Hand," www.nydailynews.com, February 24, 2009.

p. 103, par. 2, Quoted by Matthew Lee on AP News Online, February 22, 2009.

FURTHER INFORMATION

BOOKS

Abrams, Dennis. *Hillary Rodham Clinton: Politician*, New York: Chelsea House, 2009.

Guernsey, Joann Bren. *Hillary Rodham Clinton*. Minneapolis: First Avenue Editions, 2005.

Morris-Lipsman, Arlene. *Presidential Races: The Battle for Power in the United States*. Brookfield, CT: Twenty-First Century Books, 2007.

Morrison, Susan, ed. *Thirty Ways of Looking at Hillary: Reflections by Women Writers*. New York: HarperCollins, 2008.

WEBSITES

The White House Project

Website of a national, nonpartisan organization aimed at increasing women's leadership at all levels of government.

www.thewhitehouseproject.org

U.S. Department of State

Website of the U.S. Department of state, headed by Hillary Rodham Clinton.

www.state.gov

BIBLIOGRAPHY

BOOKS

Abrams, Dennis. *Hillary Rodham Clinton: Politician*. New York: Chelsea House, 2009.

Anderson, Christopher. *The American Evita: Hillary Clinton's Path to Power*. New York: William Morrow, 2004.

Bernstein, Carl. *A Woman in Charge: The Life of Hillary Rodham Clinton*. New York: Vintage Books, 2008.

Clinton, Bill. *My Life*. New York: Alfred A. Knopf, 2004.

Clinton, Hillary Rodham. *Living History*. New York: Scribner, 2003.

Cohen, Daniel. *The Impeachment of William Jefferson Clinton*. Brookfield, CT: Twenty-First Century Books, 1999.

Flinn, Susan K., ed., *Speaking of Hillary*. Ashland, OR: White Cloud Press, 2000.

Gerth, Jeff, and Don Van Natta Jr. *Her Way: The Hopes and Ambitions of Hillary Rodham Clinton*. New York: Little, Brown and Company, 2007.

Kengor, Paul. *God and Hillary Clinton: A Spiritual Life*. New York: HarperCollins, 2007.

Morrison, Susan, ed. *Thirty Ways of Looking at Hillary: Reflections by Women Writers*. New York: HarperCollins, 2008.

Sheehy, Gail. *Hillary's Choice*. New York: Random House, 1999.

PERIODICALS AND ONLINE

Atlantic Monthly Online plus extra material at www.theatlantic.com

Consortiumnews

Huffington Post

Los Angeles Times

New York Daily News

New York Times Online

New Yorker

Newsweek

Presidential Studies Quarterly

The Nation

Time magazine Online

Vanity Fair

Washington Post

Wellesley College

INDEX

Asia, visits to, 55, 101, 103
attorney general of Arkansas, Bill Clinton
as, 27

*Brown v. Board of Education of Topeka,
Kansas*, 12
Byrd, Robert, 48, 72–73

Carter, Jimmy, 27, 29
childhood
of Bill Clinton, 25
of Dorothy Howell Rodham, 9
of Hillary Clinton, **6**, 7–8
Children's Defense Fund, 22–23, 24, 29,
31–32
China, 55, 101
Chisholm, Shirley, 81
civil rights movement, 11, 12
climate change, 100
Clinton, Bill, 23, **24**, **61**, **71**
1992 presidential campaign and, **36**,
37–43
2008 presidential election and, 85–86
charitable organizations and, 74, 95
extramarital affairs and, 32–33, 37–38
as governor of Arkansas, 29–30, 34, 35
Hillary Clinton as secretary of state
and, 95–96
public speaking and, 33–34
scandal and impeachment, **58**, 59–66

Clinton, Chelsea Victoria, 29–30, **31**, **36**,
50, 56, 65, 72
concession speech, 2008 presidential
election and, 87–88
Congress, U.S., 46, **47**–48, 52, 65–66,
72–74, 75–76

Democratic Party, 14, 33–34, 84, 88–89

Edelman, Marian Wright, 22–23
education
Arkansas and, 30–31
of Bill Clinton, 25
*Brown v. Board of Education of Topeka,
Kansas*, 12
of Chelsea Clinton, 50
college education, 15, 17–22
primary and secondary education, 8,
10–11, 13, 15
law school, 22–23

Edwards, John, 83, 90–91
elections
1964 presidential election, **13**, 13, 15
1976 presidential election, 27
1988 presidential election, 33–34
1992 presidential campaign, 37–43
1992 presidential election, **36**, 37–43, **43**
1994 Congressional elections, 52
1996 presidential election, 55–56
1998 Congressional elections, 66
2000 Senate election, 70–72
2006 Senate election, 77
2008 presidential election, 9, 77, **78**,
79–91, **89**
Bill Clinton for Congress, 24–25, 26
Bill Clinton for governor, 30, 35
Equal Rights Amendment (ERA), 19
extramarital affairs, Bill Clinton and, 32–33,
37–38, 59–60

feminism, 17–18, 19, 40–41, 55
first lady
of Arkansas, 30–33
role of, 40–41
of United States, 5, **44**, 45–57, **47**, 59–67
Flowers, Gennifer, 37–38, 59
foreign relations, 93, 95, 99–101, 103
Foster, Vince, 33, 51

Giuliani, Rudy, 72, 75, **76**
Goldwater, Barry, 10, 13, 15
Goldwater Girls, 13, **13**, 15
governor of Arkansas, Bill Clinton as, 27,
29–31
grand jury, Monica Lewinsky scandal and,
63–65

health care reform, 46–49, 76, 93
Howell, Dorothy. *See* Rodham, Dorothy
Howell
human rights, 55, 97–98, 101

impeachment
Bill Clinton and, 65–66
Richard Nixon and, 25–26
independent counsel, 51
Iowa caucuses, 39, 40, 77, 82–83
Iraq War, 75, 85, 90–91

Jones, Paula, 53, 59, 60, 63

Kennedy, John F., 8, 11, 13, 25
King, Martin Luther, Jr., 11, 12, 19-20

law career, 24, 25-26, 29, 31-32
law school, 22-23
Lewinsky, Monica, 57, 59-60, **61**, 61-62, 63, 64, 65
Life magazine, **16**, 22

marriage, 26-27, 32-33
   1992 presidential campaign and, 38
   Bill's extramarital affairs and, 59
   Monica Lewinsky scandal and, 61-62, 64, 65
   running for Senator and, 69
McCain, John, 89-90, 91
McDougal, Jim and Susan, 51
Methodist Church, 11, 18-19
Myers, Dee Dee, 45, 90

name, changing, 30, 37, 45
Nixon, Richard M., 20, 25-26, **27**

Obama, Barack
   2008 presidential election and, 84, 85, 86, 88, 89, **89**, 91
   Hillary Clinton and, **83**, 95, 100-101
   Iowa caucuses and, 82, 83
Oklahoma City bombing, 54, **54**

Palin, Sarah, 89-90, 91
Perot, Ross, 43, 55-56
personal life
   Chelsea and, 29-30, 50, 56
   childhood, 7-8, 9
   dating Bill Clinton and, 23-24
   marriage, 26-27, 32-33, 37-38, 59-60
political campaigns. *See* elections
political career, of Hillary Clinton
   elections, 9, 40-43, 77, 79-91
   health care reform and, 46-49
   New York Senator, 67, 69-77
   Republican Party internship, 20
   secretary of state, 93-101, 103
   student government, 15, 19-20
political parties, 12, 14, 18-19, 73-74
politics, early interest in, 8, 10-11, 13, 15, 18
primary elections, 38-40, 83-85
public opinion
   1992 presidential campaign and, 40-42
   of Hillary Clinton, 5, 33, 72, 76, 79-80
   Monica Lewinsky scandal and, 62
   women political candidates and, 81-82

public speaking, 33-34, 38-39, 41-42, 55, 70

race relations, 11, 86
Republican Party, 14
   Barry Goldwater and, 13, 15
   Hillary Clinton and, 8, 10, 17, 20, 73-74
   Monica Lewinsky scandal and, 62
Rodham, Dorothy Howell, 7, 8, 9, 12
Rodham, Hugh, 7, 9, 10
Rodham, Hugh, Jr., 7, 52
Rose Law Firm, 27, 29, 51

Save America's Treasures Project, 57
scandals, Clinton administration and, 50-52, 53, 54, 57, 59-66
Schumer, Chuck, 66-67, 94, **97**
secretary of state, 49, 93-101, **97**, **102**, 103
Senate, U.S., 73, 75, 77, 96-99
senator, Hillary Clinton as, 67, 69-77, **74**, 93-94
September 11 terror attacks, 75, **76**
sexism, 2008 presidential election and, 90
Smith, Margaret Chase, 81
Starr, Kenneth, 51, 57, 60, 63, 65
State Department, U.S., 95, 98, 101
   See also secretary of state
student government, 15, 19-20

Teresa, Mother, 53
terrorism, 53-54, 75
Timeline, 104-105
Travelgate scandal, 50, 51
Tripp, Linda, 60

United Nations Conference on Women (Beijing), 55

vice-presidency, 2008 presidential election and, 88
Vietnam War, 18, **20**

Watergate scandal, 25-26, 51
Wellesley College, 15, 17-22
Whitewater scandal, 50-51, 52, 65-66
women political candidates, 79, 81-82, 87, 89-90
women voters, 89-90, 91
World Trade Center bombing (1993), 54
writing career, 56-57, 76-77

ABOUT THE AUTHOR

JEAN F. BLASHFIELD has been a writer of many books—more than 140 of them—on many subjects, from house plants to women's history and even murder. Most recently she has written numerous nonfiction books for young people on such subjects as science, history, biography, and government, because she particularly enjoys making confusing issues less confusing. She was the founding editor of the book department at the company that produced the Dungeons & Dragons™ role-playing game and has created three multi-volume encyclopedias. Blashfield lives in southern Wisconsin, where she raised her son and daughter.